DATE DUE

MR 0 03			
NO 18			

TIME & MONEY
Using Time Value Analysis in Financial Planning

Second Edition

Robert M. Crowe
The American College
Bryn Mawr, Pennsylvania

BUSINESS ONE IRWIN
Homewood, Illinois 60430

Production manager: Diane Palmer
Printer: The Book Press, Inc.

Library of Congress Cataloging-in-Publication Data

Crowe, Robert M.
    Time & money : using time value analysis in financial planning /
Robert M. Crowe.—2nd ed.
        p.   cm.
    Includes bibliographical references.
    ISBN 1–55623–421–X. — ISBN 1–55623–472–4 (paperback)
    1. Interest. 2. Annuities. 3. Discounted cash flow. I. Title.
II. Title: Time and money.
HG1621.C76   1991
332.024   90–41871

TO

PAT

with whom, during the past 31 years,
I have learned the enormous
time value of marriage

PREFACE

Time is money. You have undoubtedly heard that old chestnut many times. But it really is true, at least within the context of what this little book is all about. Time *costs* you money if you are a user of money now. Time can *earn* you money if you are able to wait and use your money later. So although the time value of money isn't the most important topic in the world, it is nonetheless fairly important, at least if you are someone who likes or uses money.

Some authors write books for a living. Some write them for tenure or a promotion or to avoid perishing. Some write them for the fun of it. This book has been written primarily for the last reason. Some time ago I became intrigued with the subject of the time value of money and decided I wanted to know a lot more about it. Just as I always learn a great deal from teaching my courses, so I have learned a great deal from writing this book.

There are several people who have helped me in the process of creating the first and second editions of this book, most of them colleagues of mine at The American College. Mr. Robert J. Doyle was of great help in rescuing me from some complex mathematical demons with which I was unable to cope and was invaluable in leading me through the subtleties of internal rate of return. A very bright person, Mr. Edward E. Graves, was a frequent source of neat suggestions on how best to present certain concepts. Mr. Burton T. Beam, Jr. read the entire manuscript of the first edition and made many helpful suggestions. Dr. Robert Muksian, Professor of Mathematics at Bryant College, showed amazing patience with my limited ability to understand the concept and mathematics of continuous compounding. Mrs. Nancy A. Cornman and Ms. Kathleen Maphis provided excellent typing assistance. They especially enjoyed working on the formulas. And so many students who have read the first edition helped greatly by raising penetrating questions and giving me ideas on how to explain some things more clearly. My sincere thanks to all these good people.

One of the disadvantages of being the only author of a book is that it is like playing singles in tennis. If you lose a point, there is no one else to blame it on. And so, in the unlikely event that an error or two appears somewhere in this book, I reluctantly take full responsibility for it.

Robert M. Crowe

CONTENTS

PREFACE, v

CHAPTER 1
THE CONCEPT OF THE TIME VALUE OF MONEY, 1.1
    INTRODUCTION, 1.1
    OPPORTUNITY COST, 1.1
    THE ROLE OF INTEREST, 1.1
        Simple Interest versus Compound Interest, 1.2
        Compounding versus Discounting, 1.3
    THE POWER OF COMPOUND INTEREST, 1.4
    FREQUENCY OF COMPOUNDING OR DISCOUNTING, 1.5
    MEASURING THE NUMBER OF PERIODS, 1.6
    PLAN OF THE BOOK, 1.8
    NOTES, 1.9

CHAPTER 2
FUTURE VALUE OF A SINGLE SUM, 2.1
    BASIC TIME VALUE FORMULA, 2.1
    FVSS TABLE, 2.3
    COMPUTING FVSS WITH A CALCULATOR WITH FINANCE FUNCTIONS, 2.4
        Using the HP-12C, 2.4
        Using the BA-II, 2.5
    RULE OF 72, 2.5
    COMPUTING n OR i, 2.6
    NOTES, 2.8
    PROBLEMS, 2.9
    SOLUTIONS, 2.10

CHAPTER 3
PRESENT VALUE OF A SINGLE SUM, 3.1
    USING THE TIME VALUE FORMULA, 3.1
    USING THE PVSS TABLE, 3.3
    COMPUTING PVSS WITH THE HP-12C CALCULATOR, 3.4
    COMPUTING PVSS WITH THE BA-II CALCULATOR, 3.4
    RULE OF 72, 3.4
    COMPUTING n OR i, 3.5
    PROBLEMS, 3.6
    SOLUTIONS, 3.7

CHAPTER 4
FUTURE VALUE OF AN ANNUITY OR ANNUITY DUE, 4.1
  ASSUMPTIONS, 4.1
  USING A TIME VALUE FORMULA, 4.2
  USING A TABLE TO COMPUTE FVA AND FVAD, 4.4
  USING A FINANCIAL CALCULATOR TO COMPUTE FVA AND FVAD, 4.5
    Solving FVA or FVAD on the HP-12C, 4.6
    Solving FVA or FVAD on the BA-II, 4.7
  IF NUMBER OF COMPOUNDING PERIODS EXCEEDS NUMBER OF DEPOSITS, 4.7
  SOLVING SINKING FUND PROBLEMS, 4.8
  NOTES, 4.10
  PROBLEMS, 4.11
  SOLUTIONS, 4.12

CHAPTER 5
PRESENT VALUE OF AN ANNUITY OR ANNUITY DUE, 5.1
  ASSUMPTIONS, 5.1
  USING A TIME VALUE FORMULA, 5.1
  USING A TABLE TO COMPUTE PVA AND PVAD, 5.5
  USING A FINANCIAL CALCULATOR TO COMPUTE PVA AND PVAD, 5.6
    Solving PVA or PVAD on the HP-12C, 5.6
    Solving PVA or PVAD on the BA-II, 5.7
  IF NUMBER OF DISCOUNTING PERIODS EXCEEDS NUMBER OF PAYMENTS, 5.7
  SOLVING DEBT SERVICE/CAPITAL LIQUIDATION PROBLEMS, 5.8
    Using the Table, 5.9
    Using the HP-12C or BA-II, 5.9
    Creating an Amortization Schedule, 5.10
  NOTES, 5.12
  PROBLEMS, 5.13
  SOLUTIONS, 5.14

CHAPTER 6
DEALING WITH UNEVEN CASH FLOWS, 6.1
  PRESENT VALUE OF UNEVEN CASH FLOWS, 6.1
    Using Time Value Tables, 6.1
    Using the BA-II, 6.6
    Using the HP-12C, 6.7
      Ungrouped Cash Flows at End of Year, 6.7
      Grouped Cash Flows at End of Year, 6.8
      Cash Flows at Beginning of Year, 6.9
    Payments Growing by a Constant Percentage, 6.9
  FUTURE VALUE OF UNEVEN CASH FLOWS, 6.10
    Using Time Value Tables, 6.11
    Using the BA-II, 6.12
    Using the HP-12C, 6.12
    Deposits Growing by a Constant Percentage, 6.13
  NOTES, 6.15
  PROBLEMS, 6.16
  SOLUTIONS, 6.17

CHAPTER 7
EVALUATING AN INVESTMENT THROUGH DISCOUNTED CASH FLOW ANALYSIS, 7.1
    INTRODUCTION, 7.1
    DISCOUNTED CASH FLOW TECHNIQUES DEFINED, 7.1
        Net Present Value, 7.1
        Internal Rate of Return, 7.2
        Similarity of the NPV and IRR Techniques, 7.2
    COMPUTING NET PRESENT VALUE: SIMPLE PROBLEMS, 7.2
    TOOLS FOR COMPUTING NPV: SIMPLE PROBLEMS, 7.8
    COMPUTING NET PRESENT VALUE: COMPLEX PROBLEMS, 7.9
        Ungrouped Cash Flows, 7.9
        Grouped Cash Flows, 7.10
    COMPUTING INTERNAL RATE OF RETURN, 7.10
        Using a Time Value Table, 7.11
        Using the BA-II, 7.11
        Using the HP-12C, 7.12
    PROBLEMS IN DECISION MAKING BASED ON IRR, 7.13
    COMPUTING MODIFIED INTERNAL RATE OF RETURN, 7.15
        Calculating MIRR on the HP-12C, 7.16
        Calculating MIRR on the BA-II, 7.18
    NOTES, 7.19
    PROBLEMS, 7.20
    SOLUTIONS, 7.21

CHAPTER 8
    INCREASING THE COMPOUNDING, DISCOUNTING, OR PAYMENT FREQUENCY, 8.1
        NOMINAL VERSUS EFFECTIVE INTEREST RATES, 8.1
        CALCULATING THE EFFECTIVE ANNUAL RATE, 8.2
        IMPACT OF COMPOUNDING FREQUENCY ON FUTURE VALUES, 8.4
        IMPACT OF DISCOUNTING FREQUENCY ON PRESENT VALUES, 8.4
        CALCULATING FUTURE AND PRESENT VALUES, 8.5
            Using the Effective Rate, 8.5
            Adjusting the Nominal Rate and Number of Periods, 8.6
        INTERPRETING THE RESULTS OF THE CALCULATIONS, 8.8
        ANNUITY PAYMENTS OCCURRING OTHER THAN ANNUALLY, 8.8
            Simple Annuities and Simple Annuities Due, 8.8
            Complex Annuities and Complex Annuities Due, 8.9
        NOTES, 8.12
        PROBLEMS, 8.13
        SOLUTIONS, 8.14

APPENDIX A
TIME VALUE OF MONEY TABLES, A.1
    A.1 FUTURE VALUE OF A SINGLE SUM, A.2
    A.2 PRESENT VALUE OF A SINGLE SUM, A.10
    A.3 FUTURE VALUE OF AN ANNUITY, A.17
    A.4 PRESENT VALUE OF AN ANNUITY, A.26

APPENDIX B
KEYSTROKES FOR SOLVING SELECTED TVM PROBLEMS USING THE HP-12C
CALCULATOR, B.1

APPENDIX C
KEYSTROKES FOR SOLVING SELECTED TVM PROBLEMS USING THE BA-II
CALCULATOR, C.1

APPENDIX D
TABLE OF EFFECTIVE INTEREST RATES, D.1

CHAPTER 1

THE CONCEPT OF THE TIME VALUE OF MONEY

INTRODUCTION

Why is it that when individuals take out a loan they must repay more money than they borrowed? Why is it that a supplier of materials you use in your business offers you a discount from the full amount of the invoice if you pay within 30 days? Why does the savings and loan association credit depositors' savings accounts with interest? Why is it that when you deposit a perfectly good check in your checking account the bank may deny you access to the money for a few days? Why is it inadequate for an investor to evaluate a proposed investment project on the basis of its payback period, that is, the number of years it will take for the total cash inflows from the project to equal the initial cash outlay? Why does the winner of a lottery prize of $1 million after taxes payable in $100,000 annual installments over ten years actually receive less than $1 million of value?

The answer to all of these and dozens of similar questions centers on the time value of money. These questions arise in all fields of business and personal financial planning, real estate, marketing, investments, accounting, insurance, banking, and many other fields.

Some erroneously believe that a dollar is a dollar is a dollar. The fact is that dollars to be paid or received in different time periods have different values. Ask yourself these questions. When would you rather receive your federal income tax refund check--as soon as you file your return or 3 months later? When would you rather collect the rent from the tenants in your apartment building--at the beginning of each month or at the end?

OPPORTUNITY COST

Solely on the basis of intuition most people probably would conclude, quite properly, that they would prefer to receive the money sooner rather than later. Why? Because the sooner they receive the money the sooner they can use it, either spend it or invest it, for their own benefit. If they wait for the money, they incur what economists call an "opportunity cost." The opportunity cost of an activity (in this case waiting to receive the money) is the value of the lost opportunity to engage in the best alternative activity (in this case spending or investing the money now) with the same resource (in this case the specified sum of money).

Conversely, again strictly on the basis of intuition, most would properly conclude that if they must pay out a specified sum of money, they would prefer to pay it later rather than sooner. Why? Because the longer they can delay the payment the longer they can use the money, either spend it or invest it, for their own benefit. If they pay the money early, they incur an opportunity cost.

THE ROLE OF INTEREST

Since a given sum of money due in different time periods does not have the same value, a tool is needed in order to make the different values comparable. That tool is interest, which can be viewed as a way of quantifying the opportunity cost incurred by one who waits to receive money or who gives up the opportunity to delay paying it.

For example, if you deposit $1,000 in a savings account and leave it there for one year, you expect to have more than $1,000 in the account at the end of that time. You expect your account to earn interest. You postponed the use of your money and, instead, allowed the bank to use it. You incurred an opportunity cost. The interest the bank gives you is compensation to you for having done so.

To reverse the situation, assume a loan you took out at your bank will mature in one year, at which time you are obligated to pay $10,000. If you repay the loan today, one year early, you believe you should be required to pay less than the full $10,000. If you forgo the opportunity to delay the repayment, you should be compensated in return by having the amount payable reduced.

The specific interest rate that should be used to quantify opportunity cost is made up of two components: a risk-free rate and a risk premium. At a minimum, the opportunity cost of letting someone else use your money is the rate of return you could have earned by investing it in a perfectly safe instrument. A reasonable measure of this minimum opportunity cost is the rate of interest available on 3-month U.S. Treasury bills. These bills are always available and, for all practical purposes, are risk-free. At the time of this writing, 3-month T-bills were yielding almost 8 percent on an annual basis.

In addition, most situations in which you allow someone else to use your money entail some risk of loss for you. For example, the market value of your investment instrument may decline. The purchasing power of your principal sum may be eroded by inflation. The person or organization using your funds may default on scheduled interest and principal payments. Tax laws may be changed to lower the after-tax return on your investment. These and other types of risk associated with letting someone else use your funds should be reflected in a risk premium, or add-on to the risk-free opportunity cost of money. The higher the degree of risk, the greater should be the risk premium and, therefore, the higher should be the interest rate you require.

Simple Interest versus Compound Interest

There are two ways of computing interest. *Simple interest* is computed by applying an interest rate to only an original principal sum. *Compound interest* is computed by applying an interest rate to the total of an original principal sum and interest credited to it in earlier time periods.

To illustrate the difference, assume $100 is deposited in an account which earns 6 percent simple interest per year. At the end of each year the account will be credited with $6.00 of interest. At the end of 5 years there will be $130 in the account (if no withdrawals have been made), as shown in table 1.1.

If instead the account earns 6 percent compound interest per year it will grow to a larger amount, again as shown in table 1.1. The extra $3.82 in the account when it is credited with compound interest is interest earned on previous interest earnings.

Notice the difference in the annual amount by which the account grows when compound rather than simple interest is credited. The balance grows by a constant amount, $6.00 per year, when simple interest is used. In the case of compound interest, however, the account balance grows by an increasing amount each year. The *rate* of growth, however, remains the same, 6 percent in this illustration.

Most of the day-to-day situations calling for a recognition or calculation of the time value of money involve compound interest, rather than simple interest. Hence the balance of this book will deal only with compound interest.

TABLE 1.1
Accumulation of $100 in 5 years
at 6% Simple and Compound Interest per Year

	Simple Interest			Compound Interest		
Year	Principal Sum	Interest	Ending Balance	Principal Sum	Interest	Ending Balance
1	$100.00	$6.00	$106.00	$100.00	$6.00	$106.00
2	$100.00	$6.00	$112.00	$106.00	$6.36	$112.36
3	$100.00	$6.00	$118.00	$112.36	$6.74	$119.10
4	$100.00	$6.00	$124.00	$119.10	$7.15	$126.25
5	$100.00	$6.00	$130.00	$126.25	$7.58	$133.82

Compounding versus Discounting

The process by which money today, a *present value*, grows over time to a larger amount, a *future value*, is called *compounding*. The process by which money due in the future, a *future value*, is reduced over time to a smaller amount today, a *present value*, is called *discounting*.

Figure 1.1 shows the difference between present and future value, with compound interest as the link between the two. Compounding may be viewed as a movement up the curve, while discounting may be viewed as a movement down the curve. Note also that the link between present and future value in figure 1.1 is shown as a curve, rather than as a straight line, to reflect the application of compound interest rather than simple interest. When compound interest is used, the future value rises each year by an increasing amount of money (or the present value declines by a decreasing amount of money).

Two major factors influence the shape of the curve in figure 1.1. These are (a) the number of periods over which compounding or discounting occurs, and (b) the interest rate used in the compounding or discounting process. All other things being equal, the greater the number of periods, the greater is the length of the curve. Consequently, as the number of periods is increased, the difference between the present value and the future value also increases. Similarly, all other things being equal, the greater the interest rate, the steeper is the slope of the curve. Thus as the interest rate is increased, the difference between the present value and the future value also increases.

These relationships among the number of periods (n), the interest rate (i), the future value of money (FV), and the present value of money (PV) may be summarized as follows: in compounding, FV moves in the same direction as n and i (it increases as they increase); in discounting, PV moves in the opposite direction from n and i (it decreases as they increase).

FIGURE 1.1

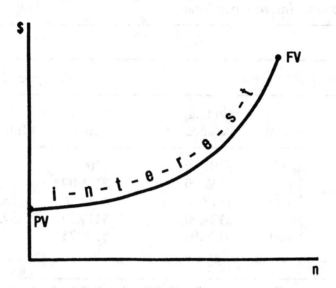

Figure 1.1. *Compound Interest as the Link between Present Value and Future Value.* This figure depicts compound interest as the link between the two values. Dollar amounts are reflected by the vertical axis and the number of periods during which compounding or discounting occurs is reflected on the horizontal axis. As one moves up the curve (compounding), the future value grows by increasing amounts. As one moves down the curve (discounting), the present value declines by decreasing amounts.

Note also that there are four key variables in virtually all problems involving the time value of money. In the simplest problems they are the number of periods, the interest rate, the present value, and the future value. In these problems, you will be given three of the variables and be called upon to solve for the fourth. In more complex time value problems the four variables are the number of periods, the interest rate, the amount of each payment in a series of payments, and either the present value or the future value. Again, you will be given three of the variables and asked to compute the fourth. And some apparently complex time value problems are simply combinations of two or more of these basic four-variable problems that are linked together.[1]

THE POWER OF COMPOUND INTEREST

Of course your concern with compound interest is not so much with the shape of a curve as with the effect that compound interest has on time value. That effect is extremely powerful, especially when a high interest rate or a long period of time is involved. For example, in the year 1980 the Consumer Price Index, a fairly good measure of the rate of inflation, rose by 13.5 percent over the preceding year. If that rate of inflation had continued throughout the decade of the 1980s, the same bag of groceries that cost $100 in 1980 would have cost about $355 in 1990! By 1995 it would have cost $668!!

One more example will help to emphasize the point. Peter Minuit is said to have purchased the island of Manhattan in the year 1626 for about $24 worth of beads. If instead of buying Manhattan he had put the $24 into a bank account paying 6 percent compound interest per year and left the money there continuously, today he would have had a bank account of approximately $41 billion, ignoring income taxes (more precisely, the balance would have been $41,385,867,534.51). You are invited to judge for yourself whether Peter made a wise purchase.

But to carry the illustration a step further, notice in table 1.2 how slowly Peter Minuit's account would have grown in the first 300 years. His money was on the flat part of the curve in figure 1.1. By 1925 he wouldn't even have become a billionaire. He really would have gotten fabulously wealthy only in the past 65 years, during which his wealth would have grown by over $40 billion. In 1991 alone it would have increased by about $2.5 billion. (Again, an important point to remember is that the *rate* of growth of his wealth was constant throughout the period, 6 percent per year. It is the *amount* of growth that accelerates under compound interest.)

TABLE 1.2
Accumulation of $24 in 365 Years
at 6% Compound Interest per Year

Year	Ending Balance
1626	$25
1675	$442
1725	$8,143
1775	$150,000
1825	$2,763,000
1875	$50,895,000
1925	$937,500,000
1975	$17,269,000,000
1990	$41,386,000,000

FREQUENCY OF COMPOUNDING OR DISCOUNTING

As you will see later in this book, there is another factor, in addition to the interest rate and the number of years, that affects the size of the present and future values of money. That factor is the frequency with which the interest rate is applied in the compounding or discounting process.

Throughout most of this book it will be assumed that the interest rate is applied once per year, which is annual compounding or discounting. You should recognize, however, that in many cases interest rates are applied several times within a year--for example, semiannually (twice a year), monthly (12 times per year), or daily (usually computed in commercial transactions by applying the interest rate 360 times per year).

All other things being equal, the greater the frequency with which compounding or discounting occurs, the greater is the effect on the growth of a future value or the decline of a present value. For example, a $1,000 principal sum which is credited with 8 percent compound interest will grow to a future value of $1,166.40 in 2 years if compounding occurs annually. If compounding occurs semiannually, on the other hand, it will grow to $1,169.86; and if compounding occurs monthly, it will grow to $1,172.89. Conversely, the present value of $1,000 due 2 years from now is $857.34 if an 8 percent annual interest rate is applied once per year. If the discounting is applied semiannually, however, the present value is only $854.80.

The explanation of why the frequency of compounding or discounting produces these results and of how to compute present and future values based on various frequencies will be deferred to Chapter 8. Meanwhile, you should assume in the text and problems for each chapter that compounding and discounting occur only once per year.

MEASURING THE NUMBER OF PERIODS

Before moving on you should note one other factor to keep in mind in the compounding or discounting process. That is the importance of being accurate in measuring the number of periods during which the compounding or discounting occurs. That, in turn, will depend on whether the process begins and ends at the beginning or the end of the periods in question.

If that sounds a bit confusing, refer back to the example of Peter Minuit in table 1.2. In that illustration year number one was 1626, and the account balance for that year was $25. That result occurred because it was assumed that $24 was deposited on January 1, 1626, the *beginning* of year one, and the account balance was computed on December 31, 1626, the *end* of year one. As a consequence, year one produced approximately $1.00 of interest.

On the other hand, what if Peter had deposited the initial $24 at the *end* of year one? Obviously, the ending account balance for that year would have been $24, and no interest would have been earned in that year.

The effect of this change in the assumption about when the initial deposit was made, whether at the start or the end of the first year, carries over into all remaining years. In table 1.2 the ending balance for 1990, some $41.3 billion, was the result of compounding for 365 years, that is, from January 1, 1626 to December 31, 1990. If Peter had begun his investment just 12 months later, at the end of 1626, compounding would have occurred for only 364 years by December 31, 1990, and his account balance would be only about $39.0 billion. In other words, the 12-month delay would have cost him over $2 billion of interest earnings. What a difference a year makes!

In order to be sure you are counting n, the number of periods, accurately in solving time value of money problems, it will be helpful to draw time lines such as those in figure 1.2 and to mark the timing of known dollar values in the problem with vertical arrows along the time line and the timing of unknown dollar values with question marks. The reason for drawing certain arrows below the line and others above it will be explained in Chapter 2. For the present you need only to recognize how the *timing* of each sum of money in a problem, both the known and unknown sums, is depicted on a time line. The upper time line, for example, depicts a case where you are to calculate the future value as of the beginning of the sixth period (which is the same as the end of the fifth period) of a deposit made at the beginning of the first period. The lower time line depicts a situation in which you are to compute the present value as of today (the start of period one) of a series of payments that will occur at the end of each of the next four periods. Time lines can be constructed for all types of time value of money problems, as will be shown frequently throughout this book.

Figure 1.2

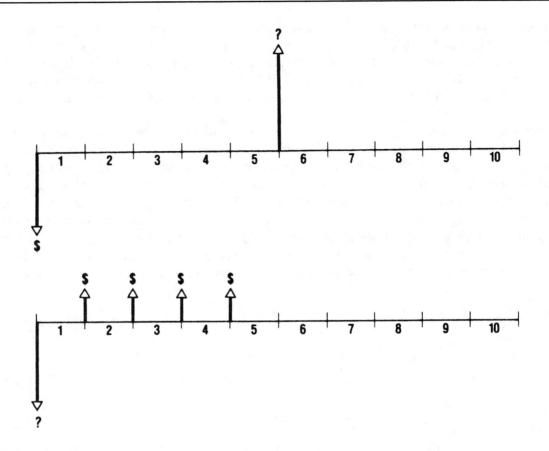

Figure 1.2 *Time Lines as Aides in Counting Number of Periods of Compounding or Discounting.* The top time line reflects a problem in which a present value is deposited at the start of period one and you are asked to solve for the future value at the start of period six, or the end of period five. The lower time line depicts a problem in which a sum of money is to be paid at the end of each of the next four periods and you are asked to solve for their present value as of the start of period one.

PLAN OF THE BOOK

The balance of this book utilizes and builds upon the basic concepts in this chapter. Emphasis is placed upon explaining *how to solve* virtually any type of problem involving the time value of money. Practical illustrations are used constantly to demonstrate principles and solution techniques. Review problems are present at the end of most chapters so that you can test your mastery of each type of problem explained.

Although this book deals with the interactions among numbers--dollars, interest rates, and time periods--you do not need a sophisticated knowledge of mathematics in order to perform any of the calculations. An ability to add, subtract, multiply, and divide, as well as an ability to raise a number to a power, will be helpful. Even these are not totally essential, however, if you have access to a calculator. (The procedure for raising a number to a power by means of a calculator is described in Appendices B and C.)

The book contains an explanation of several tools that can be used to solve time value of money problems. At the low-tech end of the spectrum, explanations are provided for solving them by directly applying mathematical formulas to the data. A rung higher up the technological ladder is the use of tables of time value factors of various types. Still higher on the ladder, two of the most popular electronic calculators with time value capabilities also are explained throughout the book.

The explanation of the various types of time value problems treated in this book proceeds in a logical progression from the least complicated to the more advanced types. Chapters 2 and 3 deal with the future value and present value of single sums of money. Chapters 4 and 5 contain explanations of the future value and present value of level streams of money payments, called annuities. Chapter 6 then takes up the future value and present value of nonlevel streams of money payments. In Chapter 7 the techniques of the preceding chapter are applied to investment decisions through an explanation of discounted cash flow analysis. Then in Chapter 8 the assumption that compounding, discounting, and payments occur only once per year is dropped and an explanation is provided on how to deal with any of the preceding types of problems where compounding, discounting, or payment frequency is greater than annual.

Now, to begin.

NOTES

1. A few problems involve five variables, of which four are known and the task is to calculate the fifth. For example, a problem might involve an initial deposit of $1,000 into a savings account, annual deposits of $100 at the end of years five, six, and seven, and compound interest earnings of 7 percent on all the deposits. The task might be to compute the account balance at the end of year 10.

CHAPTER 2

FUTURE VALUE OF A SINGLE SUM

The most frequently encountered and easiest to understand application of the time value of money concept involves the future value of a single sum. As explained in Chapter 1, determination of a future value of a sum of money entails a process of compounding, or increasing, the present value at some interest rate for some period of time. The most common example is the growth of a sum placed in an interest-bearing savings account. Recall, for example, that in table 1.1 a $100 deposit made today (a present value) will grow to $133.82 (a future value) at the end of 5 years at 6 percent compound interest.

BASIC TIME VALUE FORMULA

The basic formula for computing the future value of a single sum of money, from which all other time value formulas are derived, is the following:

$$FVSS = PVSS (1 + i)^n$$

where

$FVSS$ = the future value of a single sum

$PVSS$ = the present value of a single sum

i = the compound annual interest rate, expressed as a decimal

n = the number of years during which compounding occurs

That is, add the interest rate (expressed as a decimal) to one, and raise this sum to a power equal to the number of years during which the compounding occurs. Then multiply this by the present value of the single sum, or deposit, in question to compute the future value of that single sum.

For example, assume that $5,000 is placed on deposit today in an account that will earn 9 percent compound annual interest. To what amount will this sum of money grow by the end of year seven? The problem is depicted on a time line in figure 2.1 below.

It is important, both conceptually and mathematically, to recognize that in every time value of money problem there is an implicit tradeoff over time of a sacrifice for a gain, a cost for a benefit. For example, you may be willing to loan money to a friend today (a cost or cash outflow in the present) in order to be repaid a larger amount later (a benefit or larger cash inflow in the future). Throughout this book the nature of this tradeoff will be pointed out over and over. For purposes of consistency among the time lines used to depict various types of problems to be discussed, present values will be depicted below the line, as will periodic cash outflows. Future values and periodic cash inflows will be shown as above-the-line factors.

FIGURE 2.1

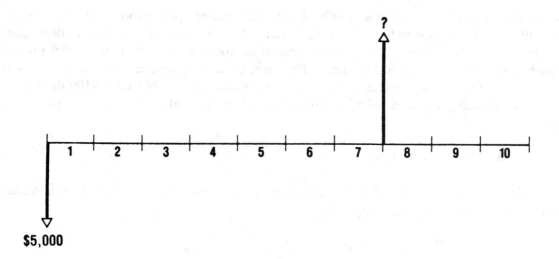

Figure 2.1. *Time Line Depiction of FVSS Problem*. This time line depicts a problem in which a known single sum, $5,000, is deposited today, at the start of year one, and you are to calculate its future value as of the end of year seven. The time line also illustrates the basic tradeoff present in all time value of money problems. Here the tradeoff is a cash outflow today (the deposit, shown below the time line) for a larger cash inflow later (the account balance at the end of the seventh year), shown above the time line).

To return to the problem at hand, then, the $5,000 that is placed on deposit today represents a present value. The amount to which it will grow at 9 percent compound annual interest by the end of the seventh year is the future value. The basic time value formula can be used to compute the solution as follows:

$$FVSS = PVSS\ (1 + i)^n$$

$$= \$5,000\ (1.09)^7$$

$$= \$5,000\ (1.828039)$$

$$= \$9,140.20$$

To reiterate a point made in Chapter 1, note what would happen to FVSS if i were more than 9 percent or if n were more than 7 years. In either case the quantity $(1 + i)^n$ would be larger than 1.828039, so that when multiplied by $5,000 the FVSS would be larger than $9,140.20. That is, future value increases as the interest rate or the number of years increases, and it falls as either of them is lowered.

FVSS TABLE

The process of raising $(1 + i)$ to the nth power can be time consuming and tedious, as well as filled with possibilities for making arithmetic errors. To simplify the task, a table has been constructed showing the value of $(1 + i)^n$ for various rates of interest and numbers of periods. (See table A.1 in Appendix A.) Excerpts from that table are presented below. All that needs to be done is to select the correct factor from the table and multiply it by the present value of the sum in question to compute its future value.

TABLE 2.1
Future Value of a Single Sum Factors

n/i	7%	8%	9%	10%	11%
1	1.0700	1.0800	1.0900	1.1000	1.1100
2	1.1449	1.1664	1.1881	1.2100	1.2321
3	1.2250	1.2597	1.2950	1.3310	1.3676
4	1.3108	1.3605	1.4116	1.4641	1.5181
5	1.4026	1.4693	1.5386	1.6105	1.6851
6	1.5007	1.5869	1.6771	1.7716	1.8704
7	1.6058	1.7138	1.8280	1.9487	2.0762
8	1.7182	1.8509	1.9926	2.1436	2.3045
9	1.8385	1.9990	2.1719	2.3579	2.5580
10	1.9672	2.1589	2.3674	2.5937	2.8394
11	2.1049	2.3316	2.5804	2.8531	3.1518
12	2.2522	2.5182	2.8127	3.1384	3.4985
13	2.4098	2.7196	3.0658	3.4523	3.8833
14	2.5785	2.9372	3.3417	3.7975	4.3104
15	2.7590	3.1722	3.6425	4.1772	4.7846

For example, look down the 9 percent column to the row for seven periods, and the factor 1.8280 is found, virtually the same amount as was computed in the preceding example when the quantity 1.09 was raised to the seventh power.[1] What that computation and the table have disclosed is that if the present value of a single sum is one, its future value at 9 percent for seven periods is 1.8280. Since the present value of the single sum in the illustration is not one but $5,000, the factor for one must be multiplied by $5,000 to produce the future value of that sum of money, namely, $9,140.20.

Take another look at table 2.1. Note that as you move from left to right across a particular row in the table, to higher and higher interest rates, the FVSS factor increases. Also, as you move from top to bottom down a particular column in the table, to higher and higher numbers of periods, the FVSS factor increases. Once again, FVSS rises as either i or n rises, and vice versa.

COMPUTING FVSS WITH A CALCULATOR WITH FINANCE FUNCTIONS

A powerful tool for solving time value of money problems is the financial calculator. This type of calculator greatly speeds the task of solving these problems, especially the more complex ones described later in this book. Two of the most popular electronic calculators with finance functions currently on the market are the HP-12C Programmable Financial Calculator produced by Hewlett-Packard Company and the BA-II Executive Business Analyst™ calculator produced by Texas Instruments Incorporated. In this book an explanation will be furnished showing how to solve on these two calculators each type of time value of money problem as it is encountered.[2] The individual keystrokes in each sequence of calculator keystrokes shown throughout the book are separated by commas. If at some point in a sequence you key in an incorrect number, you can correct the mistake by immediately pressing the CLX key on the HP-12C or the ON/C key on the BA-II.

Using the HP-12C

To use the HP-12C calculator to solve future value of a single sum problems, turn the machine on by pressing the ON key in the lower left corner of the keyboard. Next, depress the yellow f key[3] and the CLX key, which has REG printed above it. This serves to clear any data that may have been stored earlier in the financial and several other "registers" (memory units) of the machine. If you wish to clear only the financial registers, press the yellow f key and the x≷y key, which has FIN printed above it, instead. (It is a good idea to get into the habit of clearing the memory of the calculator each time you use it to solve a problem.) Next, depress the yellow f key and the number 2. This will cause the machine to display dollar values carried to two decimal places, which is the level of precision to be used for dollar values throughout this book. (As will be explained later, other values, such as those for n and i, will sometimes be entered or displayed with other numbers of decimal places.)

The next steps are to enter the three known values in the FVSS problem, namely, PVSS, n, and i. These may be entered in any order. The language of the HP-12C, however, includes an important convention that reflects the cost-benefit tradeoff in all time value problems referred to earlier. This convention, called the cash flow sign convention, requires that at least one (and usually only one) value to be entered into the calculator in a time value problem be entered as a negative number. This is accomplished through use of the CHS (change sign) key in the top row of the keyboard. If this is not done, the cash flow sign convention usually causes solutions to problems to be displayed as negative numbers. For purposes of consistency, present values will be entered or displayed as negative numbers. Also, as will be explained later, the amount of a payment that constitutes a cash outflow in a series of payments in some types of problems will be entered or displayed as a negative number on the HP-12C.

Now take a moment to review the keys on the left-hand portion of the top row of the keyboard. These keys (n, i, PV, PMT, FV), as well as the yellow and blue functions they activate and the CHS key, will be used in solving various types of time value of money problems.

To return to the example given earlier, assume you wish to know the amount to which a single sum of $5,000 will grow in 7 years at 9 percent compound interest. Since i is 9, press the 9 key, then the i key. Since n is 7, depress 7, then n. And since the sum of money today is $5,000, press 5000, CHS (since it is the present value), and PV. Finally, press FV and the answer, $9,140.20, will appear on the display.[4]

If you wish to change one of the data items in the problem, you may do so without reentering all the information. For example, if you wish to recalculate the same problem with a 12 percent interest rate, simply press 12, i, and FV. The new amount, $11,053.41, appears on the display.

Using the BA-II

In order to solve time value of money problems using the BA-II calculator, turn the machine on and clear the display screen by pressing the ON/C key in the upper right-hand corner of the keyboard. Next, clear the calculator of any previous information contained in the mode "registers" (memory units). This is accomplished by pressing the key labeled 2nd in the upper left-hand corner and the key next to it, which has CMR (clear mode registers) printed above it.[5] (It is a good idea to get into the habit of clearing the memory of the calculator each time you use it to solve a problem.) Next press the FIX key and the number 2. This will cause the machine to round numbers to two decimal places, which is the level of precision to be used for dollar values throughout this book. (As will be explained later, other values, such as those for n and i, will sometimes be entered or displayed with other numbers of decimal places.) Then inform the machine that you will be using its finance functions. To do so, press the 2nd and FIX keys once or twice until the label FIN appears on the display.

Take a moment to review the keys in the second row from the top of the keyboard. These keys (N, %i, PMT, PV, and FV), along with the 2nd and DUE keys in the top row, will be used in solving various types of time value of money problems.

To return to the example given earlier, assume you wish to know the amount to which a single sum of $5,000 will grow in 7 years at 9 percent compound interest. These three known values should be entered into the calculator. They may be entered in any order. Since the interest rate is 9, press 9 and %i. Then enter the number of years involved by pressing 7 and N. Next is the sum of money today. Press 5000 and PV. Finally, press 2nd and FV and the answer, $9,140.20, appears on the display.[6]

If you wish to change one of the data items in the problem, you may do so without reentering all the information. For example, if you wish to recalculate the same problem with a 5-year compounding period, simply press 5, N, 2nd, and FV. The new amount, $7,693.12, appears on the display.

RULE OF 72

Occasionally you may find it unnecessary to obtain a precise measurement of the effect of interest in the compounding process and that a rough estimate of the future value of a single sum will suffice. In such cases a simple device called the "rule of 72" may be found useful.

The rule of 72 is a quick method for estimating how long it will take for a sum to double in value at various compound interest rates. In this method the number 72 is divided by the applicable interest rate expressed as a whole number. The quotient is the number of periods in question.[7]

For example, at a compound annual interest rate of 9 percent, a $100 principal sum will double in value and reach $200 in approximately (72 ÷ 9 =) 8 years. It will double again and reach $400 in approximately another 8 years and double still again, reaching $800, at the end of approximately 8 more years. At a compound annual interest rate of 6 percent, on the other hand, the growth of the principal sum will be much slower, since it will take about (72 ÷ 6 =) 12 years for each doubling to occur.

Remember that the rule of 72 produces only approximations, and that for most purposes you will want to be more precise. Moreover, the amount of imprecision produced by using the rule of 72 increases as the interest rate and the principal sum are increased. (As a partial corrective measure, some prefer to divide the interest rate into the number 78 for interest rates of 20 percent or more.) More precise methods for computing the effects of compounding than the rules of 72 or 78 will be used in the balance of this book.

In some types of future value of a single sum problems FVSS and PVSS are known, as well as either i or n. The task in such cases is to use the three known values to compute the fourth.

For example, assume that you plan to deposit $1,200 in a savings account and withdraw the money when the account balance reaches $1,500. How long will you have to wait if the annual compound interest rate on the account is 7.5 percent?

The reader who is mathematically talented can solve this problem through the basic time value formula by substituting the known values in it as shown below, and then solving for n.[8]

$$1500 = 1200 \, (1.075)^n$$

Alternatively, if you happen to have an FVSS table with a column of factors for an interest rate of 7.5 percent, read down the column to find the factor closest to 1.25, which is $1500 \div 1200$. Then read across to the years column to determine the approximate n. (From table A.1 on page A.3 in the Appendix you can find that the approximate n is 3 years.)

It should be obvious that neither the formula nor the table provides a quick and precise method for dealing with the problem of computing n. An electronic calculator with finance functions, however, can compute n as readily as it computes FVSS.

On the HP-12C, for example, after clearing the machine as described above, enter the three known values in any order and solve for the fourth. Press 7.5, i, 1500, FV, 1200, CHS (in accordance with the machine's cash flow sign convention), PV, and n. The answer, 4.00 years, appears on the display.

Actually this is an incomplete answer because of a design limitation of the HP-12C in dealing with this type of problem. If the answer is not an integer, or whole number, the HP-12C usually rounds the answer up to the next higher integer. This in effect means that the final year contained in the displayed value for n is actually only a partial year. (The HP-12C rounds down to the next lower integer if the portion of n to the right of the decimal point is less than .005, resulting in a slight understatement of the actual n.) If you wish a more precise value for n on the HP-12C, the best approach is to use the formula in note 8 at the end of this chapter together with the log function of the calculator.

The BA-II provides a more precise answer to the problem of calculating n than does the HP-12C. After clearing the machine's display and memory and setting it for financial functions and, for example, four decimal places as described earlier, press 7.5, %i, 1500, FV, 1200, PV, 2nd, and N. The more exact answer, 3.0855 years, appears on the display.

Instead of solving for n in a time value problem, in many cases the task will be to solve for i. For example, what compound annual interest rate must you earn on your money if you have $6,000 to invest today and wish to have $10,000 in 5 years? Solving this type of problem is complex mathematically. Hence an explanation involving the use of a formula will not be attempted here.

Use of the FVSS table to compute an interest rate is more feasible, at least for simple problems. The approach in the present example is to look across the row for the number of periods in the problem, five, until you find the FVSS factor closest to 1.6667, which is the FVSS, $10,000, divided by the PVSS, $6,000. On page A.4 in the Appendix the factors 1.6474 and 1.6851 appear in the 5-year row. Look at the interest rates at the top of these columns and you can properly conclude that the interest rate in this problem is somewhere between 10.5 percent and 11.0 percent. Perhaps that is a sufficiently close approximation for some purposes. Alternatively, you could use a process of interpolation to get closer to the exact answer. Much greater convenience and precision in solving for i, however, are possible with a financial calculator.

On the HP-12C, for example, set the number of decimal places to four and enter the three known values in any order: 10000, FV, 5, n, 6000, CHS, PV, and i. After a few seconds the answer appears as 10.7566 percent. Or on the BA-II, after you make sure the memory is clear set the number of decimal places to four and press 5, N, 6000, PV, 10000, FV, 2nd, and %i to produce the answer, 10.7566 percent. (As with the HP-12C, any order in which you choose to enter the three known variables is acceptable.)

NOTES

1. You should not be concerned with small differences among answers produced by the use of the table versus the formula or a calculator. Differences of a few cents often arise because of the lesser precision of the tables in the rounding process.

2. The descriptions provided for the solution of problems using the HP-12C and the BA-II are for educational purposes only and should not be construed as an endorsement of them by either the author or the publisher. Neither the HP-12C nor the BA-II is the most sophisticated calculator marketed by the two manufacturers. However, the HP-12C is relatively inexpensive and can be used to solve any type of time value of money problem described in this book. The BA-II is a bit less expensive than the HP-12C but lacks the capability for solving most uneven cash flow problems as described in Chapters 6 and 7. At the time of this writing, Texas Instruments was developing an upgraded version of its BA-II calculator, but it was not sufficiently developed to permit inclusion of it in this book.

3. Several keys on the HP-12C calculator perform more than one function. This is accomplished by means of the yellow f key and blue g key on the bottom row of the keyboard. Pressing yellow f and a key causes the key to perform the function printed in yellow above that key. Pressing blue g and a key causes the key to perform the function printed in blue on the lower edge of that key. For example, press the 9, ENTER, 2, and y^x keys. The number 81, which is 9 squared, appears on the display. Now press CLX, 9, ENTER, blue g, and the same y^x key. The number 3, which is the square root of 9, appears on the display. Pressing the blue g key switched the function to be performed by the y^x key from raising the number to a power (y^x), in this case squaring it, to finding its square root ($\sqrt{x}$).

4. For your convenience, Appendix B lists the keystrokes to be used in solving the most common types of time value of money problems on the HP-12C.

5. Several keys on the BA-II keyboard perform two separate functions. The first function is that printed on the key. The second is that printed directly above it. This latter function is performed by pressing the key marked 2nd in the upper left-hand corner of the keyboard, followed by the key in question. For example, press the keys 9 and x^2. The answer, 81, which is 9 squared, is displayed. Now press ON/C, 9, 2nd, and the same x^2 key. The answer, 3, which is the square root of 9, is displayed. Pressing 2nd switched the function to be performed by the x^2 key from squaring the number (x^2) to finding its square root ($\sqrt{x}$).

6. For your convenience, Appendix C lists the keystrokes to be used in solving the most common types of time value of money problems on the BA-II.

7. The rule of 72 can be used for purposes of discounting as well as for compounding, as will be explained in Chapter 3. In this case the result of dividing the number 72 by the interest rate is the approximate number of periods it will take to produce a present value equal to one half the original sum.

8. Specifically, the formula is as follows:

$$n = \frac{\log \left[\dfrac{FVSS}{PVSS} \right]}{\log \ (1 + i)}$$

2.8

PROBLEMS

1. A real estate appraiser has advised you that the value of homes in your neighborhood has been rising at a compound annual rate of about 6 percent in recent years. On the basis of this information, what is the value today of the home you bought 7 years ago for $119,500?

2. According to the rule of 72, approximately how long will it take for a sum of money to double in value if it earns a compound annual interest rate of 4 percent?

3. Although you have made no deposits or withdrawals from your emergency fund savings account at the bank, the account balance has risen during the past 3 years from $15,000 to $17,613.62.

   (a) What has been the compound annual interest rate that the bank has been crediting to your account?

   (b) At that rate, when will your account balance reach $20,000?

SOLUTIONS

(Note: Solutions to most of the problems at the end of each chapter have been calculated with the answers rounded to two decimal places for dollar values and four decimal places for interest rate values and values of n. Your solutions may vary slightly from those presented due to rounding differences.)

1. The house should be worth about $179,700 today. In table A.1, the factor to be used is 1.5036. $119,500 x 1.5036 = $179,680.20. Or using a financial calculator, $119,500 compounded at 6 percent for 7 years produces FV = $179,683.82.

2. At a 4 percent compound annual interest rate, according to the rule of 72 it will take about 18 years for a sum of money to double in value, because $72 \div 4 = 18$. A more precise answer, found by means of a financial calculator, is n = 17.6730.

3. (a) Your account has been credited with 5.5 percent compound annual interest. $17,613.62 \div $15,000 = 1.1742. In table A.1 in the 3-year row the factor 1.1742 is in the 5.5% column. Or using a financial calculator with $15,000 as the PV, $17,613.62 as the FV, and 3 as the n, i = 5.5000%.

   (b) Your account balance will reach $20,000 in a little more than 2 years. $20,000 \div 17,613.62 = 1.1355. In table A.1 in the 5.5% column, this FVSS factor is between those for 2 and 3 years, and is closer to that for 2 years. Through the use of a process of interpolation or a financial calculator, you can find that the precise n = 2.3731.

CHAPTER 3

PRESENT VALUE OF A SINGLE SUM

The preceding chapter dealt with the question of compounding, of computing how a known single sum of money accumulates over time to an unknown future value. In the present chapter the question is reversed. Given the future value of a single sum of money, what is it worth today? What is its present, or discounted, value?

For example, assume that in 4 years it will be necessary to spend $125,000 to replace an asset that is wearing out. How much money should be on hand today in an account earning 10 percent compound interest in order to reach that goal? Or assume that you are scheduled to receive a $75,000 lump sum distribution from a trust 5 years from now. For how much would you sell that right today (if you are permitted to do so) if interest rates are 7 percent? (See figure 3.1.)

USING THE TIME VALUE FORMULA

You learned in Chapter 2 that FVSS can be found through the formula

$$FVSS = PVSS (1 + i)^n$$

Students of elementary algebra will recognize that this formula can be rearranged to

$$PVSS = FVSS \left[\frac{1}{(1 + i)^n} \right] = \frac{FVSS}{(1 + i)^n}$$

That is, FVSS multiplied by the mathematical reciprocal of $(1 + i)^n$, which is the same as dividing FVSS by $(1 + i)^n$, produces the PVSS. Discounting is thus the reverse of compounding. When compounding you should multiply the known sum by $(1 + i)^n$, whereas in discounting you should multiply it by the reciprocal of that quantity (or divide it by that quantity).

In the top line of figure 3.1, then, you need to have $125,000 in 4 years for replacement of the wearing out asset. If you can earn 10 percent compound interest, you should set aside today a total of a little over $85,000. That is,

$$PVSS = \$125,000 \left[\frac{1}{(1.10)^4} \right] = \frac{\$125,000}{(1.10)^4}$$

$$= \frac{\$125,000}{1.4641}$$

$$= \$85,376.68$$

This amount, accumulating at 10 percent compound annual interest, will grow to the necessary $125,000 when it is needed in 4 years.

And the present value of that $75,000 trust fund distribution due to be received in 5 years, if the interest rate is 7 percent, is a little more than $53,000.

$$\text{PVSS} = \$75,000 \left[\frac{1}{(1.07)^5}\right] = \frac{\$75,000}{(1.07)^5}$$

$$= \frac{\$75,000}{1.4026}$$

$$= \$53,472.12$$

FIGURE 3.1

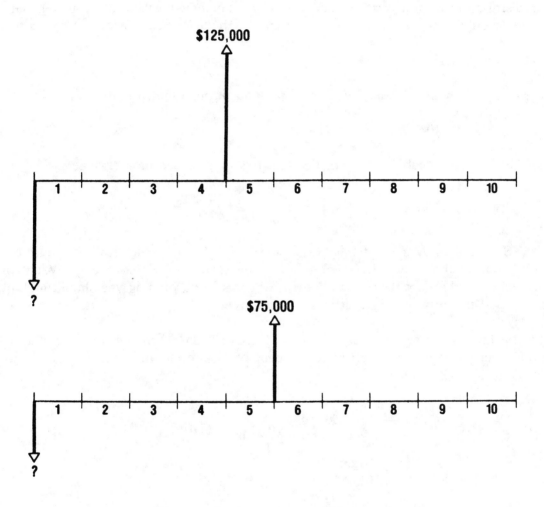

$125,000

$75,000

Figure 3.1 *Time Line Representation of PVSS Problems.* The time line on the top represents a problem in which you are asked to determine the present value of a $125,000 single sum due 4 years hence. In the time line on the bottom the problem is to compute the PVSS when the FVSS is $75,000 due in 5 years.

Note the effect of a change in i or n on PVSS. If either of these is increased, the denominator of the formula increases and, when it is divided into FVSS, the resulting PVSS declines. For example, the present value of the $75,000 trust fund distribution due in 5 years is only $46,569.39 if the interest rate used in discounting is 10 percent; it is still smaller, $34,987.87, if it is due in 8 years and the interest rate is 10 percent. A decrease in either i or n, on the other hand, causes PVSS to rise.

USING THE PVSS TABLE

The calculation of present values by means of the formula is as tedious, time consuming, and susceptible to errors as is the calculation of future values. To simplify the process of computing PVSS, a table has been constructed showing the value of $1 \div (1 + i)^n$ for various rates of interest and numbers of years. (See table A.2 in Appendix A.) Excerpts from that table are presented below.

Table 3.1
Present Value of a Single Sum Factors

n/i	7%	8%	9%	10%	11%
1	0.9346	0.9259	0.9174	0.9091	0.9009
2	0.8734	0.8573	0.8417	0.8264	0.8116
3	0.8163	0.7938	0.7722	0.7513	0.7312
4	0.7629	0.7350	0.7084	0.6830	0.6587
5	0.7130	0.6806	0.6499	0.6209	0.5935
6	0.6663	0.6302	0.5963	0.5645	0.5346
7	0.6227	0.5835	0.5470	0.5132	0.4817
8	0.5820	0.5403	0.5019	0.4665	0.4339
9	0.5439	0.5002	0.4604	0.4241	0.3909
10	0.5083	0.4632	0.4224	0.3855	0.3522
11	0.4751	0.4289	0.3875	0.3505	0.3173
12	0.4440	0.3971	0.3555	0.3186	0.2858
13	0.4150	0.3677	0.3262	0.2897	0.2575
14	0.3878	0.3405	0.2992	0.2633	0.2320
15	0.3624	0.3152	0.2745	0.2394	0.2090

This table, it should be remembered, is a direct by-product of table 2.1, which showed FVSS factors. All that was done to produce table 3.1 was to divide each factor in table 2.1 into one; that is, each PVSS factor is the reciprocal of the FVSS factor for the same n and i.

To compute the present value of a single sum, select the appropriate factor from the PVSS table and multiply it by the future value of the sum in question. For example, to find the present value of $125,000 needed in 4 years and discounted at a 10 percent interest rate, look down the 10% column to the row for four periods. The factor, .6830, is multiplied by $125,000 to produce the answer, $85,375. And the present value of $75,000 to be received in 5 years and discounted at 7 percent is ($75,000 x .7130 =) $53,475.

Once again, review table 3.1 to see the effect of changes in n and i on PVSS. As you move down any interest rate column to higher levels of n, the PVSS factor, and hence PVSS, declines. And as you move across the row for any number of periods to higher levels of i, the PVSS factor, and hence PVSS, declines.

COMPUTING PVSS WITH THE HP-12C CALCULATOR

The task of computing the present value of a future sum of money is greatly simplified by the HP-12C financial calculator. As explained in Chapter 2, clear the machine and set it to display two decimal places. The next step is to enter the three known values into the machine in any order. Then press the PV button to solve for the present value of the single sum in question.

For example, assume you own a zero-coupon bond that will mature in 13 years, at which time it will pay you $1,000. Meanwhile, it will pay you nothing. What would you sell the bond for today if you believe you could invest the proceeds elsewhere and earn 9 percent compound interest?

Enter 9, i, 13, n, 1000, and FV. The calculator is now programmed to compute the present value of the $1,000 due to be received in the future. Depress the PV key and the answer, $326.18, is displayed. (Remember that the HP-12C's cash flow sign convention referred to in Chapter 2 shows the answer as a negative number if all the data are entered as positive numbers.) That is, if you were to invest $326.18 at 9 percent compound interest, you would have $1,000 at the end of 13 years. (You may wish to verify this by computing the FVSS of $326.18 as explained in Chapter 2.)

COMPUTING PVSS WITH THE BA-II CALCULATOR

If you wish to use the BA-II calculator to compute the present value of a single sum, clear the memory and set the machine to perform finance functions and to display two decimal places, as was explained in Chapter 2. Then enter the three known values into the calculator in any order. Finally, press the 2nd and PV keys to compute the present value of the single sum in question.

For example, assume that you own a zero-coupon bond that will mature in 6 years, at which time it will pay you $1,000. Meanwhile, it will pay you nothing. What would you sell the bond for today if you believe you could invest the proceeds elsewhere and earn 11 percent compound interest?

Enter 1000, FV, 11, %i, 6, and N. The calculator is now programmed to compute the present value of the $1,000 due to be received in the future. Depress the 2nd and PV keys and the answer, $534.64, is displayed. That is, if you were to invest $534.64 at 11 percent compound interest for the next 6 years, you would have $1,000 at the end of that time. (You may wish to verify this by computing the FVSS of $534.64 as explained in Chapter 2.)

RULE OF 72

In Chapter 2 the rule of 72 was presented as a quick method for estimating how long it will take for a sum of money to double in value. It can also be used to estimate how long it will take for a sum of money to halve in value. For example, if an average annual inflation rate of 8 percent should be experienced over an extended period, a person's $50,000 salary would fall in purchasing power to $25,000 in approximately (72 ÷ 8 =) 9 years (if the salary remains at $50,000).

As is true of future value problems, it is sometimes useful to be able to compute either n or i, given the other and given FVSS and PVSS. For example, assume that you owe $5,000 to be paid in a lump sum in 2 years. The lender offers to accept $4,750 today in satisfaction of the loan. Should you accept the offer? The answer depends at least partly on the rate of return (interest) the lender is effectively offering you.

This can be determined by using table A.2 in the Appendix. First divide the present value, $4,750, by the future value, $5,000. The answer is .9500. Then look across the row for two periods and find the PVSS factor closest to .9500. That factor is .9518, which is in the 2.5% column. Hence the lender is offering you about 2.5 percent per year to pay the loan early. That hardly sounds like a bargain!

Alternatively, you can use a financial calculator. Set your HP-12C to display four decimal places. Then enter 5000, FV, 4750, CHS (again, present values should be entered as negative numbers), PV, 2, and n. Then press the i key to produce the answer, 2.5978 percent. Or set your BA-II to display four decimal places. Then press 2, N, 4750, PV, 5000, and FV. Then depress the 2nd and %i keys. The lender has offered you a compound annual rate of return on your money of 2.5978 percent.

To reverse this illustration, if you insist on obtaining an 8 percent compound annual rate of return on your money, when would you be willing to pay the lender $4,750 to discharge your $5,000 debt? If you wish to use table A.2 to find the number of periods, look down the 8% column to find the factor nearest to .9500. The closest the table comes is to .9259 in the row for one period. This means you would not be willing to pay off the loan more than one year early.

As was explained in Chapter 2, the HP-12C provides only an approximate answer to this type of problem. Press 4750, CHS, PV, 5000, FV, 8, and n to produce the answer, one year. The BA-II is more precise. After setting it to display four decimal places, press 8, %i, 4750, PV, 5000, and FV. Now press 2nd and N to compute the answer, 0.6665. That is, if you repay the $5,000 loan about 8 months early (two thirds of one year) for $4,750, your compound annual rate of return will be 8 percent.

PROBLEMS

1. There is an attractive piece of undeveloped land that you are considering purchasing. You think that in 5 years it will sell for $30,000. What would you pay for it today if you want to earn a compound annual rate of return of 12 percent on your investment?

2. Your personal net worth has risen in the past 4 years from $110,000 to $260,000 due to your shrewd investing. What has been the compound annual rate of growth of your net worth during this period?

3. You hope to accumulate $45,000 as a down payment on a vacation home in the near future.

   (a) If you can set aside $38,000 now in an account that will be credited with 8 percent compound annual interest, how long will it take until you have the needed down payment?

   (b) What if you can get 9 percent per year on your money?

SOLUTIONS

1. You should be willing to pay about $17,000 for the property today. In table A.2, the factor to be used is 0.5674. $30,000 x 0.5674 = $17,022. Or with a financial calculator, $30,000 discounted at 12 percent for 5 years produces PV = $17,022.81.

2. Your net worth has grown at a compound annual rate of almost 24 percent. $110,000 ÷ $260,000 = .4231. In table A.2 in the 4-year row, the closest factor is .4230, which is in the 24.0% column. Through a process of interpolation or the use of a financial calculator, you could calculate the precise amount, i = 23.9924%.

3. (a) It will take a little over 2 years to accumulate the down payment. $38,000 ÷ $45,000 = .8444. In table A.2 in the 8% column, this value lies between the factors for 2 and 3 years, and is closer to the 2-year factor. By interpolation or use of a financial calculator, you could find that the precise n = 2.1969. (Note, however, that the HP-12C produces an imprecise n = 3.)

    (b) With a higher rate, the waiting period is shortened to just under 2 years. In the 9% column of table A.2, .8444 lies between the factors for 1 and 2 years and is closer to that for 2 years. If you interpolate or use a financial calculator you will see that n = 1.9619.

CHAPTER 4

FUTURE VALUE OF AN ANNUITY OR ANNUITY DUE

Chapter 2 contained an explanation of how to compute the future value of a *single* sum placed on deposit or paid into an account credited with compound interest. The present chapter builds upon and expands that case to deal with the calculation of the future value of a *series* of deposits or payments. For example, if $300 is deposited, or paid, into an account *each year* and is credited with 11 percent compound annual interest, how much will be in the account at the end of 6 years?

This type of problem will be referred to as a future value of an annuity (FVA) or a future value of an annuity due (FVAD) problem. An annuity is a series of payments of equal amounts made at the *end* of each of a number of periods. An annuity due is a series of payments of equal amounts made at the *beginning* of each of a number of periods.[1]

There are many personal and business situations where sums of money are invested periodically. Some corporations, for example, make available payroll deduction plans whereby employees may save for a desired objective by having a stipulated amount withheld from each paycheck and invested in U.S. government savings bonds. Many individuals deposit a pre-established amount each week or month in Christmas Club or Vacation Club accounts at banks or credit unions. Many wage earners and self-employed individuals deposit funds each year in Individual Retirement Accounts (IRAs) or Keogh plans at banks, thrift institutions, brokerage firms, insurance companies, or mutual funds. Tax-advantaged employee benefit programs such as 401(k) and tax-deferred annuity plans are vehicles for employees to make periodic deposits, often matched by employer contributions, to save for retirement. Corporate sinking fund contributions to accumulate money for the purchase of fixed assets are another example of the annuity principle.

ASSUMPTIONS

To simplify the solution of FVA and FVAD problems, it will be assumed in this chapter that the deposits or payments are made annually. This assumption will be modified later in this book. (See Chapter 8.) Also, it will be assumed that the deposits all earn the same rate of compound interest, though obviously each earns it for a different length of time.

In that connection, it is particularly important in problems such as those discussed in this chapter to be accurate in measuring the length of time during which each deposit earns compound interest. One possible assumption is that the deposits are made at the beginning of each year (an annuity due); the other is that they are made at the end of each year (an annuity). The difference between the two future values, all other things being equal, can be quite large.

For example, assume five annual payments of $1,000 each earn 7 percent compound interest. At the end of the fifth year the future value of these periodic payments will be $6,153.29 if they are made at the beginning of each year versus only $5,750.74 if they are made at the end. The $402.55 difference between the two future values, FVAD and FVA, is due to the fact that each deposit earns one more year of interest under the first assumption than under the second. That is, when deposits are made at the start of each year the first deposit earns interest for 5 years rather than 4, the second for 4 years rather than 3, etc., and the last deposit earns interest for one year rather than none. (See figure 4.1.)

FIGURE 4.1

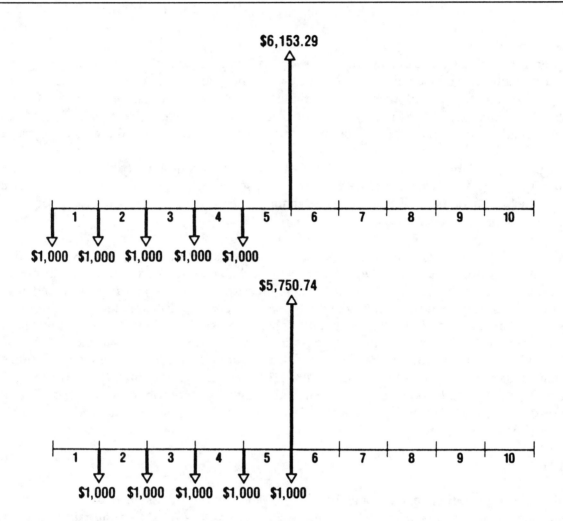

Figure 4.1. *Time Line Representation of FVAD and FVA Problems.* The top time line depicts a problem in which $1,000 deposits are made at the beginning of each of 5 years (an annuity due), and the problem is to determine the future value as of the end of the fifth year. In the lower time line the problem is the same in all respects except that the deposits are made at the end of each of the 5 years (an annuity).

USING A TIME VALUE FORMULA

Problems calling for calculation of the future value of an annuity or annuity due can be viewed as collections of FVSS problems. Each annuity payment or deposit is a single sum which earns compound interest for a different number of years. Hence the FVA or FVAD is really the sum of a series of FVSS calculations.

To illustrate, assume that $100 is deposited at the end of each of 4 years and earns 5 percent compound annual interest. What is the total future value of these deposits at the end of the fourth year? The first deposit earns interest for 3 years (that is, from the end of year one till the end of year four). Hence its future value is

$$FVSS = PVSS(1 + i)^n$$

$$= \$100 \ (1.05)^3$$

$$= \$100 \ (1.1576)$$

$$= \$115.76$$

The future value of the second deposit, which earns interest for 2 years, is

$$FVSS = PVSS(1 + i)^n$$

$$= \$100 \ (1.05)^2$$

$$= \$100 \ (1.1025)$$

$$= \$110.25$$

The future value of the third deposit, which earns interest for one year, is

$$FVSS = PVSS(1 + i)^n$$

$$= \$100 \ (1.05)^1$$

$$= \$105.00$$

And the future value of the fourth deposit is $100, the same as its present value, because it earns no interest. Thus the FVA in this illustration is ($115.76 + $110.25 + $105.00 + $100.00 =) $431.01.

If, on the other hand, the deposits had been made at the beginning of each year, their future values would have been as follows:

1st	$100 \ (1.05)^4$ =	\$121.55
2nd	$100 \ (1.05)^3$ =	115.76
3rd	$100 \ (1.05)^2$ =	110.25
4th	$100 \ (1.05)^1$ =	<u>105.00</u>
FVAD		\$452.56

As an alternative to the foregoing approach of summing the future value of each of the separate deposits, the same result can be achieved in one step by using a somewhat more complex formula for cases where the deposits are made at the end of each year.

$$FVA = \left[\frac{(1 + i)^n - 1}{i}\right] \text{ (amount of one deposit)}$$

In the previous illustration,

$$FVA = \left[\frac{(1.05)^4 - 1}{.05}\right] (\$100)$$

$$= \left[\frac{.2155}{.05}\right] (\$100)$$

$$= \$431.01$$

For cases in which the deposits are made at the beginning of each year, the same formula may be used, but with one important modification. To reflect the fact that each deposit will be credited with one extra year of interest, it is necessary to multiply the result of the preceding formula by $(1 + i)$. That is, if deposits are made at the beginning of each year, the formula becomes

$$FVAD = (1 + i)\left[\frac{(1 + i)^n - 1}{i}\right] \text{ (amount of one deposit)}$$

$$= (1.05) \left[\frac{(1.05)4 - 1}{.05}\right] (\$100)$$

$$= (1.05) \left[\frac{.2155}{.05}\right] (\$100)$$

$$= (1.05) (\$431.01)$$

$$= \$452.56$$

A simple way to keep the FVAD calculation in mind is to calculate FVA through the end-of-year formula above. If the problem is a beginning-of-year case, multiply the result by $(1 + i)$ to produce the FVAD.

USING A TABLE TO COMPUTE FVA AND FVAD

Those who are somewhat less mathematically inclined may prefer to avoid memorizing and applying the formulas contained in the preceding section. They will be heartened to learn, undoubtedly, that most of the work has already been done for them, and that the results of computing the quantity

$$\frac{(1 + i)^n - 1}{i}$$

for various rates of interest and numbers of periods appear in a table. (See table A.3 in Appendix A.) Excerpts from that table appear below. To compute the FVA, the future value of a series of periodic payments made at the end of each year, simply multiply the appropriate factor in this table by the amount of one of the payments. To compute FVAD, multiply the result of the foregoing calculation by $(1 + i)$.

For example, assume that an individual deposits $2,000 at the end of each year for 13 years in an IRA account earning 11 percent compound interest per year. How much will be in the account at the end of the thirteenth year? Locate the FVA factor in the 11% column, row 13. The future value of these periodic deposits will be ($2,000 x 26.2116 =) $52,423.20. If, on the other hand, the 13 deposits are made at the beginning of each year, the FVAD will be 11 percent higher, because each deposit will earn one extra year's interest. Hence the FVAD is ($2,000 x 26.2116 x 1.11=) $58,189.75.

TABLE 4.1
Future Value of an Annuity Factors

n/i	7%	8%	9%	10%	11%
1	1.0000	1.0000	1.0000	1.0000	1.0000
2	2.0700	2.0800	2.0900	2.1000	2.1100
3	3.2149	3.2464	3.2781	3.3100	3.3421
4	4.4399	4.5061	4.5731	4.6410	4.7097
5	5.7507	5.8666	5.9847	6.1051	6.2278
6	7.1533	7.3359	7.5233	7.7156	7.9129
7	8.6540	8.9228	9.2004	9.4872	9.7833
8	10.2598	10.6366	11.0285	11.4359	11.8594
9	11.9780	12.4876	13.0210	13.5795	14.1640
10	13.8164	14.4866	15.1929	15.9374	16.7220
11	15.7836	16.6455	17.5603	18.5312	19.5614
12	17.8885	18.9771	20.1407	21.3843	22.7132
13	20.1406	21.4953	22.9534	24.5227	26.2116
14	22.5505	24.2149	26.0192	27.9750	30.0949
15	25.1290	27.1521	29.3609	31.7725	34.4054

USING A FINANCIAL CALCULATOR TO COMPUTE FVA AND FVAD

As with the types of time value problems discussed in earlier chapters, an electronic calculator with finance functions is a very useful tool for solving FVA and FVAD problems. Among the advantages of the calculator over formulas or tables are its great speed, its reduced likelihood of error, and the great range of values for n and i that it can handle.

Solving FVA or FVAD on the HP-12C

To use the HP-12C, clear the memory units and set the calculator to display two decimal places. In annuity and annuity due problems you will be using a new key on the top row of the keyboard, PMT (payment), to reflect the fact that a series of deposits is involved, rather than a single sum. Also, when solving a problem involving a series of payments or deposits you must *always* remember to instruct the calculator as to whether the payments or deposits will be made at the end of each period (FVA) or at the beginning (FVAD). This will be accomplished through use of the blue g key and the blue END or blue BEG function in the top row of the keyboard.

To illustrate, assume that a young couple deposits $5,000 today and at the start of each of the next 4 years in a savings account to accumulate a down payment for a house. If the account is credited with 8 percent compound interest per year, how much of a down payment will the couple have 5 years from now? (See the time line depiction of this type of problem in figure 4.2.)

FIGURE 4.2

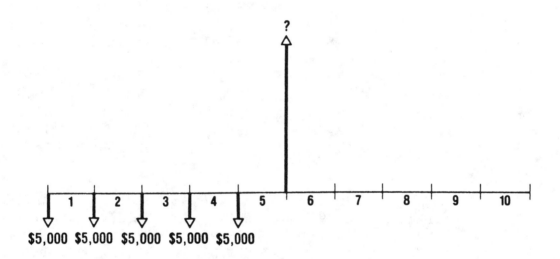

Figure 4.2. *Time Line Representation of FVAD Problem.* This time line depicts a 5-year annuity due. The problem is to determine the FVAD as of the end of the fifth year.

Depress the following keys to reflect the known information: 5000, CHS (because, as was noted in Chapter 2, deposits that represent cash outflows are treated as negative numbers according to the cash flow sign convention), PMT, 8, i, 5, n, blue g, BEG (because the deposits are made at the start of each of the 5 years), and FV. The answer, the FVAD, $31,679.65, appears on the display. If the deposits had been made at the end of each of the 5 years, the keystrokes would be identical except for the substitution of END for BEG after blue g. The answer under this new assumption, the FVA, would be $29,333.00. You can produce this solution simply by pressing blue g, END, and FV, rather than reentering all the information in the problem.

Solving FVA or FVAD on the BA-II

If you wish to use the BA-II, clear the memory units and set the calculator to display two decimal places. In annuity and annuity due problems you will be using a new key on the second row of the calculator keyboard, PMT (payment), to reflect the fact that a series of deposits is involved, rather than a single sum. Also, when solving a problem involving a series of payments or deposits you must *always* remember to instruct the calculator as to whether the payments or deposits will be made at the end of each period (FVA) or at the beginning (FVAD). This will be accomplished through the use of the 2nd key for end-of-period problems or the DUE key for beginning-of-period cases. (The DUE key is located in the top row of the keyboard.)

To illustrate, assume that a married couple deposits $5,000 today and at the start of each of the next 4 years in a savings account to accumulate funds for their young daughter's college education. If the account is credited with 8 percent compound interest per year, how much of a college fund will the couple have 5 years from now? (See the time line depiction of this problem in figure 4.2)

Depress the following keys to reflect the known information: 5000, PMT, 5, N, 8, %i, DUE (because the deposits are made at the start of each of the 5 years), and FV. The answer, the FVAD, $31,679.65, appears on the display. If the deposits had been made at the end of each of the 5 years, the keystrokes would be identical except for the substitution of 2nd for DUE before FV. The answer under this new assumption, the FVA, would be $29,333.00. You can produce this solution simply by pressing 2nd and FV, rather than reentering all the information in the problem.

IF NUMBER OF COMPOUNDING PERIODS EXCEEDS NUMBER OF DEPOSITS

Sometimes a problem will be encountered in which the number of periods during which compounding occurs exceeds the number of periods during which deposits are made. For example, assume that $500 is to be deposited at the end of each of the next 6 years in an account earning 8 percent compound annual interest. How much will be in the account at the end of 10 years? (See figure 4.3.)

The simplest way to solve a problem of this type is to treat it as two separate problems and combine the results. The first step is to compute the FVA; the second is to treat that value as a single sum and compute its FVSS.

In this illustration, the FVA for 6 years and 8% interest, based on, for example, the factor from table A.3, is

$$FVA = \$500 \ (7.3359)$$

$$= \$3,667.95$$

The FVSS at 8 percent interest at the end of the remaining 4 years, using the factor from table A.1, is

$$FVSS = \$3,667.95 \ (1.3605)$$

$$= \$4,990.25$$

FIGURE 4.3

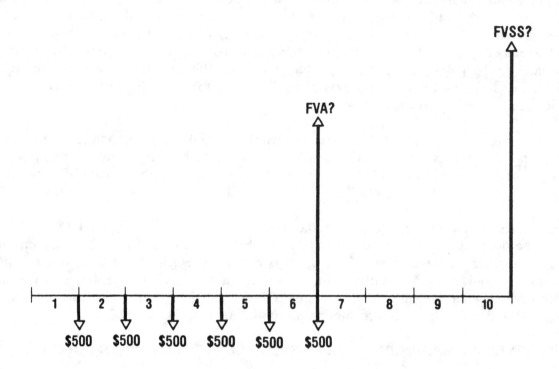

Figure 4.3. *Time Line Representation of Problem where Number of Compounding Periods Exceeds Number of Deposits.* In this time line level payments are made at the end of each of 6 years. The future value of that annuity as of the end of the sixth year is then left as a single sum to accumulate until the end of the tenth year.

SOLVING SINKING FUND PROBLEMS

So far in this chapter you have learned how to compute the future value of a series of payments or deposits when the number of payments, the rate of interest, and the size of each payment are known. Sometimes, however, the facts are different, and it is the size of the periodic payment which is the unknown of the four key elements. This is often called a sinking fund payment problem.

For example, assume that a business wishes to accumulate $10,000,000 by the end of 3 years in order at that time to retire some of its outstanding mortgage bonds. The company plans to make three annual deposits, beginning today, into a sinking fund which will earn 9 percent compound interest. The question: how large must each of the deposits be in order to reach the target amount in 3 years?

Although the answer can, of course, be found by rearranging the FVA or FVAD formula and solving for the amount of the deposit, the use of a table or financial calculator is much more efficient. Hence only those methods will be explained here.

If you wish to use the FVA table, simply divide the target amount, the future value of the deposits, by the factor for the proper i and n. When calculating the FVA or FVAD, you *multiplied* the proper factor by one of the deposits. When calculating the amount of one of the deposits, you should *divide* the FVA or FVAD by the proper factor.

Since in the present illustration the sinking fund payments are to be made at the beginning of each year, you must first convert the FVA factor in table A.3 for 3 years, 9%, which is 3.2781, into an FVAD factor. This is done by multiplying it by 1.09. The resulting PVAD factor, 3.5731, is then divided into the desired FVAD, $10,000,000, to produce the size of each deposit that will be needed to reach that goal, namely, $2,798,690.21. Three deposits of this amount, one made today and the others at the beginning of each of the next 2 years, all earning 9 percent compound annual interest, will grow to approximately $10,000,000 by the end of the third year.

Using a financial calculator is even more efficient than using table A.3, as well as more precise because of a lesser problem of rounding. On the HP-12C, for example, press the following keys: 10000000, FV, 9, i, 3, n, blue g, BEG, and PMT. The answer, $2,798,667.50, is displayed on the screen (with a minus sign, in accordance with the cash flow sign convention). On the BA-II, the same answer is found by pressing 10000000, FV, 9, %i, 3, N, DUE, and PMT.[2]

Variations from the foregoing sinking fund problem are problems in which the task is to compute n, the number of deposits that will be required, or i, the interest rate that must be earned on the deposits, in order to reach the target amount. For such purposes a financial calculator is the most effective tool.

Assume, for example, that you wish to accumulate $10,000 for a dream vacation in Tahiti and that you can afford to save $1,200 per year, beginning a year from now, toward that objective. If your savings earn 10 percent compound annual interest, how long will you have to wait before you can buy your airline tickets? On the BA-II press the following keys: 10000, FV, 10, %i, 1200, PMT, 2nd, and N. The answer is 6.3596 years.[3]

On the other hand, if you insist on waiting only 5 years before going to Tahiti with your $10,000, what compound annual interest rate must you earn on your periodic deposits? On the HP-12C, press 10000, FV, 1200, CHS, PMT, 5, n, blue g, END, and i. The answer, hardly encouraging, will appear after a few seconds of running time as 25.7839 percent. The BA-II provides no happier an answer. Press 10000, FV, 1200, PMT, 5, N, 2nd, and %i to produce the answer after a few seconds, 25.7839 percent.[4]

1. In some fields, such as insurance, the terms "annuity" and "annuity due" are used to refer to a series of payments the value of which includes both compound interest *and mortality* factors. Such annuities are more accurately referred to as *life* annuities or *life* annuities due.

2. If the sinking fund payments were to be made at the end of each of the 3 years, the methods of solving the problem would be slightly different. If the table is used, divide $10,000,000 by the factor in table A.3 without first multiplying the factor by 1.09. On the HP-12C, press END after blue g, rather than BEG. On the BA-II, press 2nd instead of DUE. The precise answer is $3,050,547.57. The larger deposits are necessitated, of course, by the fact that each deposit will earn interest for one year less under the end-of-year assumption.

3. As was explained in Chapter 2, the HP-12C is less precise than the BA-II in solving for n. In this case, the HP-12C would give an answer of 7 years. Use of the FVA table without interpolating also produces only a rough approximation of the answer. Divide the $10,000 future value by the $1,200 payment to produce a factor of 8.3333. Then in the 10% column find the factor closest to this number. That factor is 7.7156, which appears in the row for six periods. The answer to the problem is, thus, somewhere between 6 and 7 years.

4. Use of a table to try to solve this problem points out another limitation of tables as a solution tool. They may not extend to sufficiently high (or low) interest rates to cover all situations. In the present illustration, divide the $10,000 future value by the $1,200 payment to produce a factor of 8.3333. Then in the five-period row find the factor closest to this number. That factor is 8.2070, which appears in the 25.0% interest column. The answer to the problem, therefore, is something more than 25%, though how much more is not possible to determine because this table does not show a rate higher than 25.0%.

PROBLEMS

1. You have decided that, beginning one year from now, you are going to deposit your $1,200 annual dividend check in a savings account at the credit union to build up a retirement fund. The account will be credited with 6 percent compound annual interest.

   (a) If you plan to retire 18 years from now, how much will be in the account at that time?

   (b) If you should decide to retire 3 years earlier than that, how much will be in the account?

2. The round-the-world trip you and your spouse intend on taking on your 25th wedding anniversary, 6 years from now, will cost $22,000.

   (a) How much should you set aside each year, beginning today, to reach that objective if you can earn 9 percent compound annual interest on your money?

   (b) How will the size of the annual deposit needed be affected if you can earn only 8 percent compound annual interest?

3. You have just started depositing in an education fund account for your newly-born son $2,000 at the beginning of each year. How much will be in the account

   (a) after 11 years if it earns 8.5 percent compound annual interest?

   (b) after 13 years if it earns 8.5 percent compound annual interest?

   (c) after 18 years if it earns 7.5 percent compound annual interest and you discontinue making deposits after the fifth deposit?

SOLUTIONS

1. (a) There will be about $37,087 in the account at the end of 18 years. In table A.3 the correct FVA factor is 30.9057. $1,200 x 30.9057 = $37,086.84. Or if you use a financial calculator, FVA = $37,086.78.

   (b) At the end of 15 years the account balance will be almost $27,931. From table A.3 the FVA factor of 23.2760 is multiplied by $1,200 to produce FVA = $27,931.20. If you use a financial calculator, the more precise answer is FVA = $27,931.16.

2. (a) You should set aside approximately $2,683 now and at the beginning of each of the next 5 years in order to reach the target amount. In table A.3 the factor for 9%, 6 periods is 7.5233. To convert this to an FVAD factor, 7.5233 is multiplied by 1.09 to produce 8.2004. The target amount, $22,000, is divided by 8.2004 to produce an annuity due payment of $2,682.80. On a financial calculator, the beginning of year PMT = $2,682.78.

   (b) If only 8% compound annual interest is earned, the size of the needed annual deposit rises to about $2,777. The factor is 7.3359 x 1.08 = 7.9228. Dividing $22,000 by 7.9228 = $2,776.80. Or on the calculator, the beginning of year PMT = $2,776.79.

3. (a) After 11 years at 8.5% there will be approximately $37,099 in the account. In table A.3 the correct FVA factor is 17.0961. The correct FVAD factor is 17.0961 x 1.085 = 18.5493. $2,000 x 18.5493 = $37,098.54 FVAD. On the calculator, FVAD = $37,098.50.

   (b) After 13 years at 8.5% there will be about $48,198 in the account. From table A.3 the factor is 22.2109 x 1.085 = 24.0988. $2,000 x 24.0988 = $48,197.60 FVAD. On the financial calculator, replacing 11 with 13 as n produces FVAD = $48,197.73.

   (c) At the end of 5 years there will be about $12,488 in the account. The table A.3 factor is 5.8084 x 1.075 = 6.2440. Multiplying $2,000 by this factor produces $12,488.06 as the FVAD. This amount, carried forward as a single sum for 13 more years at 7.5%, (see table A.1) will grow to $12,488.06 x 2.5604 = $31,974.43. If you use a financial calculator, $12,488.04 will be in the account at the end of 5 years. Clear the machine and reenter this as the PV, with 7.5 as the i and 13 as the n. FV = $31,974.54.

CHAPTER 5

PRESENT VALUE OF AN ANNUITY OR ANNUITY DUE

Chapter 3 contained an explanation of how to calculate the present value of a *single* sum due or needed at some time in the future. This chapter expands on that case and deals with the question of how to compute the present value of a *series* of level future payments. This type of problem will be referred to as a present value of an annuity (PVA) problem if the payments are to be made at the end of each year or as a present value of an annuity due (PVAD) problem if they are to be made at the beginning of each year.[1]

To illustrate the type of problem that is the concern of this chapter, assume that an installment loan is to be repaid to you through six annual payments of $1,000 each beginning a year from now. For how much would you be willing to sell the promissory note today if you believe you can earn 8 percent compound annual interest on your money in some other investment outlet? What is the present value of this 6-year annuity discounted at 8 percent?

ASSUMPTIONS

As was true in the preceding chapter concerning the future value of a series of payments, it will be assumed in this chapter on present value that each payment is made annually. This assumption will be dropped later in the book. (See Chapter 8.) In addition, it will be important to specify in each example whether the annuity payments are made at the end or at the beginning of each year. The difference in the answer can be substantial. For example, an 8-year, $1,000 annuity discounted at 6 percent has a PVA of $6,209.79, versus a PVAD of $6,582.38. (See figure 5.1.)

USING A TIME VALUE FORMULA

The basic formula for computing the present value of a single sum can also be used to compute the present value of an annuity or an annuity due. All that is needed is to calculate the PVSS for each annuity payment separately and total the results.

For example, assume that as part of a divorce settlement a father has been ordered to deposit a lump sum in trust sufficient to provide child support payments for his son. The child support payments are to be $5,000 per year for 4 years, beginning one year from today. If the amount placed in trust can be assumed to earn 7 percent compound annual interest, how much should the father place in the trust today?

Through the formula described in Chapter 3, the present value of each separate payment can be found. The amount to be deposited today would be equal to the combined present value of the four payments.

FIGURE 5.1

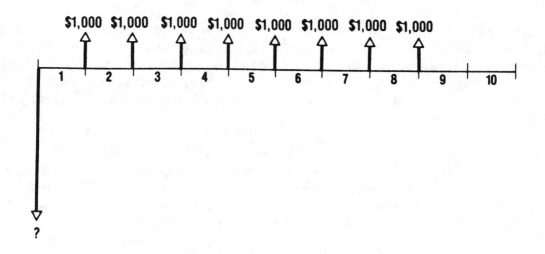

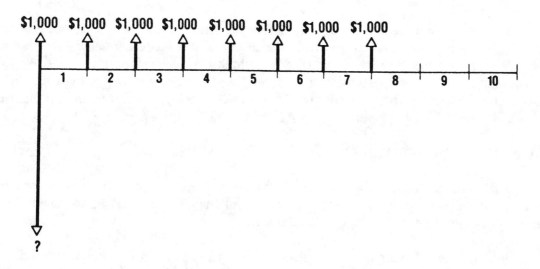

Figure 5.1. *Time Line Representation of PVA and PVAD Problems.* The upper time line depicts a case in which 8 annual annuity payments of $1,000 are to be made beginning in one year and the problem is to compute the PVA. The lower time line depicts an 8-year annuity due, in which $1,000 payments are made at the start of each year, and the problem is to compute the PVAD.

Specifically, the present value of the first payment, to be made in one year, would be

$$PVSS = FVSS \left[\frac{1}{(1 + i)^n} \right]$$

$$= \$5,000 \left[\frac{1}{(1.07)^1} \right]$$

$$= \$5,000 \, (.9346)$$

$$= \$4,673.00$$

The present value of the second, third, and fourth payments would be as shown below:

$$2\text{nd} = \$5,000 \left[\frac{1}{(1.07)^2} \right] = \$5,000 \left[\frac{1}{1.1449} \right] = \$5,000 \, (.8734) = \$4,367.00$$

$$3\text{rd} = \$5,000 \left[\frac{1}{(1.07)^3} \right] = \$5,000 \left[\frac{1}{1.2250} \right] = \$5,000 \, (.8163) = \$4,081.50$$

$$4\text{th} = \$5,000 \left[\frac{1}{(1.07)^4} \right] = \$5,000 \left[\frac{1}{1.3108} \right] = \$5,000 \, (.7629) = \$3,814.50$$

The sum of these present values, the PVA, would be ($4,673.00 + $4,367.00 + $4,081.50 + $3,814.50 =) $16,936.00. That amount, placed on deposit today at 7 percent compound annual interest, will be just enough (well, within $.07 of just enough) to provide four annual payments of $5,000 each beginning in one year. To verify this, examine what would happen to the account each year.

Year	Beginning Balance	Interest Earnings	Amount Withdrawn	Ending Balance
1	$16,936.00	$1,185.52	$5,000.00	$13,121.52
2	$13,121.52	$ 918.51	$5,000.00	$ 9,040.03
3	$ 9,040.03	$ 632.80	$5,000.00	$ 4,672.83
4	$ 4,672.83	$ 327.10	$5,000.00	($ 0.07)

If, on the other hand, the four annual payments were to be made beginning immediately, the PVAD would be as follows:

5.3

1st	PVSS $= \$5,000$	$\left[\dfrac{1}{(1.07)^0}\right]$	$= \$5,000$	(1.0000)	$= \$\ 5,000.00$
2nd	PVSS $= \$5,000$	$\left[\dfrac{1}{(1.07)^1}\right]$	$= \$5,000$	$(.9346)$	$= \$\ 4,673.00$
3rd	PVSS $= \$5,000$	$\left[\dfrac{1}{(1.07)^2}\right]$	$= \$5,000$	$(.8734)$	$= \$\ 4,367.00$
4th	PVSS $= \$5,000$	$\left[\dfrac{1}{(1.07)^3}\right]$	$= \$5,000$	$(.8163)$	$= \underline{\$\ 4,081.50}$

$$\text{PVAD} \qquad\qquad\qquad \$18,121.50$$

Why would a larger amount need to be deposited in trust if the payments are to begin immediately? The total interest earnings would be lower because each withdrawal to make the child support payments would occur a year earlier than under the end-of-year assumption.

As an alternative to the foregoing approach of finding PVA or PVAD by summing the present value of each of the separate annuity payments, the same result can be achieved in one step by using the following, somewhat more complex formula.

$$\text{PVA} = \left[\dfrac{1 - \left[\dfrac{1}{(1+i)^n}\right]}{i}\right] \text{(amount of one payment)}$$

Note that this formula should be used only for the case where the annuity payments are made at the end of each year.

In the child support illustration, then,

$$\text{PVA} = \left[\dfrac{1 - \left[\dfrac{1}{(1.07)^4}\right]}{.07}\right] (\$5,000)$$

$$= \left[\dfrac{1 - \left[\dfrac{1}{1.3108}\right]}{.07}\right] (\$5,000)$$

$$= \left[\dfrac{.2371}{.07}\right] (\$5,000)$$

$$= (3.3871) \ (\$5,000)$$

$$= \$16,935.50$$

For cases in which the payments are to be made at the beginning of each year, the same formula may be used, but with one important modification. To reflect the fact that each payment will earn one fewer year of interest before it is distributed, it is necessary to multiply the result of the preceding formula by $(1 + i)$. That is, if the payments are made at the beginning of each year, the formula becomes

$$PVAD = (1 + i) \left[\frac{1 - \left[\frac{1}{(1 + i)^n} \right]}{i} \right] \text{(amount of one payment)}$$

$$= (1.07) \left[\frac{1 - \left[\frac{1}{(1.07)^4} \right]}{.07} \right] (\$5,000)$$

$$= (1.07) \left[\frac{.2371}{.07} \right] (\$5,000)$$

$$= (1.07) \ (\$16,935.50)$$

$$= \$18,120.99$$

As was done in converting from FVA to FVAD, then, the way to compute PVAD is to compute PVA, and then multiply the result by $(1 + i)$.

USING A TABLE TO COMPUTE PVA AND PVAD

By this time it should come as no surprise to the reader that the factors generated through the foregoing PVA formula for various rates of interest and numbers of years have already been calculated. They appear in table A.4 in Appendix A. Excerpts from that table are presented below. To compute the PVA, simply multiply the appropriate factor in this table by the amount of one of the annuity payments. To compute the PVAD, multiply the PVA by $(1 + i)$.

For example, assume that you have won the lottery and will be receiving \$15,000 per year, beginning in one year, for the next 10 years. What is the present value of your prize if interest rates are at 9 percent? From table 5.1 or A.4, the PVA factor for 10 years, 9% is 6.4177. This factor is multiplied by the amount of one of the payments, \$15,000, to produce the PVA, \$96,265.50.

One of the few things in life that would be nicer than the lottery prize you won would be if the 10 annual payments were to begin immediately, rather than 12 months from now. In this case, the PVAD would be 9 percent higher; that is, \$15,000 x 6.4177 x 1.09 = \$104,929.40.

5.5

TABLE 5.1
Present Value of an Annuity Factors

n/i	7%	8%	9%	10%	11%
1	0.9346	0.9259	0.9174	0.9091	0.9009
2	1.8080	1.7833	1.7591	1.7355	1.7125
3	2.6243	2.5771	2.5313	2.4869	2.4437
4	3.3872	3.3121	3.2397	3.1699	3.1024
5	4.1002	3.9927	3.8897	3.7908	3.6959
6	4.7665	4.6229	4.4859	4.3553	4.2305
7	5.3893	5.2064	5.0330	4.8684	4.7122
8	5.9713	5.7466	5.5348	5.3349	5.1461
9	6.5152	6.2469	5.9952	5.7590	5.5370
10	7.0236	6.7101	6.4177	6.1446	5.8892
11	7.4987	7.1390	6.8052	6.4951	6.2065
12	7.9427	7.5361	7.1607	6.8137	6.4924
13	8.3577	7.9038	7.4869	7.1034	6.7499
14	8.7455	8.2442	7.7862	7.3667	7.1909
15	9.1079	8.5595	8.0607	7.6061	7.1909

USING A FINANCIAL CALCULATOR TO COMPUTE PVA AND PVAD

Use of an electronic calculator with finance functions greatly eases the task of calculating the present value of an annuity or of an annuity due. The calculator is faster, less likely to produce mistakes, and allows for the selection of more values for n and i than are likely to be found in most present value tables.

Solving PVA and PVAD problems involves use of the same special keys and functions (on the HP-12C, the PMT, blue END, and blue BEG; on the BA-II, the PMT, 2nd, and DUE) as were described in connection with the solution of FVA and FVAD problems. Readers who have not already read Chapter 4 should do so before continuing with this chapter.

Solving PVA or PVAD on the HP-12C

Assume that a woman receives $6,000 each year from a trust. She is interested in obtaining a cash sum with which to buy a fancy new sports car. Her cousin has offered to buy from her now the present value of the next four annuity payments (the first of which will be made one year from now) discounted at 8 percent compound annual interest. How much will the woman receive if she accepts the offer?

If you are using the HP-12C, clear the memory units and set the calculator to display two decimal places. Then depress the following keys to enter the known information: 6000, CHS (because we are the payments will be made at the end of each year). The calculator is now programmed to compute the PVA. Depress the PV key and the answer, $19,872.76, is displayed on the screen.

If the facts of the problem were revised so that the four annual payments from the trust were to begin immediately, the procedure for solving it would be identical except that the BEG key would be pressed instead of the END key. You can solve it now by pressing blue g, BEG, and PV. The answer, the PVAD, is $21,462.58.

Solving PVA or PVAD on the BA-II

Assume that several years ago the owner of a small business borrowed $10,000 from a relative and agreed to repay the loan in 10 equal annual installments of $1,500. Six payments now remain to be made, the first of which is due in one year. The business owner now would like to pay off the remainder of the debt. What sum should the business owner propose to the lender as a payoff figure if money is presently worth 7 percent?

If you are using the BA-II, clear the memory units, set the calculator to display two decimal places, and set it to perform finance functions. Then depress the following keys to enter the known information: 1500, PMT (because the problem involves a series of payments rather than a single sum), 6, N, 7, %i, and 2nd (because the payments will be made at the end of each year). The calculator is now programmed to compute the PVA. Depress the PV key and the answer, $7,149.81, is displayed on the screen.

If the facts of the problem were revised so that the remaining six annual payments were to be made beginning immediately, the procedure for solving it would be identical except that the DUE key would be pressed instead of the 2nd key. You can solve it now by pressing DUE and PV. The answer, the PVAD, is $7,650.30.

IF NUMBER OF DISCOUNTING PERIODS EXCEEDS NUMBER OF PAYMENTS

Sometimes a problem will be encountered in which the number of periods during which discounting is to occur exceeds the number of periods during which annuity payments are to be made. For example, what is the present value at a 7 percent compound annual interest rate of an income stream consisting of five annual payments of $2,000 each, the first of which will be made 3 years from now? (See the time line depiction of this type of problem in figure 5.2.)

The simplest way to solve a problem of this type, called a deferred annuity problem, is to treat it as two separate problems and combine the results. The first step is to compute the PVA; the second is to treat that value as a single sum and compute its PVSS.

In the present illustration the PVA for 5 years and 7%, based on the factor from table A.4, is

$$PVA = \$2,000 \ (4.1002)$$

$$= \$8,200.40$$

FIGURE 5.2

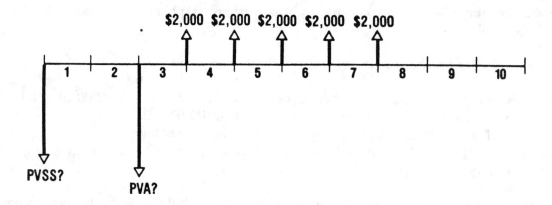

Figure 5.2. *Time Line Depiction of PVA or PVAD Problems Where Discounting Period Exceeds Payment Period.* This time line depicts a case in which five annual payments of $2,000 each are to be made beginning in 3 years. The problem, which is to determine the present value of the income stream, can be divided into two parts. First determine the present value of the annuity as of the start of the annuity period, which is the beginning of year three. Then compute the present value of that single sum as of today, 2 years earlier.

The PVSS at 7 percent for the value of an annuity that commences in *2 years* (even though the first payment will not be made until the end of *3 years*), based on the factor from table A.2, is

$$PVSS = \$8,200.40 \ (.8734)$$

$$= \$7,162.23$$

Note that in this solution a PVA was calculated and then discounted as a single sum for 2 additional years. The same result can be achieved if the problem is viewed as entailing the calculation of a PVAD and then discounting that single sum for 3 additional years. (Re-examine figure 5.2 to verify that a 5-year PVA discounted for an additional 2 years is identical to a 5-year PVAD discounted for an additional 3 years.)

SOLVING DEBT SERVICE/CAPITAL SUM LIQUIDATION PROBLEMS

Thus far in this chapter you have seen how to compute the present value of a stream of equal payments when the number of payments, the rate of interest, and the size of each payment are known. Sometimes, however, it is the size of the periodic payment which is the unknown of the four key elements. A frequently encountered problem of this type is that of determining the amount of money necessary to liquidate a debt through periodic loan repayments. A similar problem is to determine how large a periodic withdrawal from a sum of capital can be in order to liquidate that sum over a given number of years.

In installment loans such as those used to finance the purchase of a house or automobile, each level periodic payment, called the debt service, consists of some repayment of the principal and some payment of interest on the remaining unpaid principal. Given the initial size of the loan, the interest rate, and the number of payments to be made, the problem is to compute the size of each required payment.[2] Such a debt service problem can be solved using PVA and PVAD factors in a manner analogous to that for solving sinking fund problems using FVA and FVAD factors as explained in Chapter 4.

For example, assume that a real estate mortgage for $50,000 bearing an 11 percent interest rate is to be repaid in 15 equal annual installments, the first to be made in one year. The question: how large must each annual installment payment be?

Although the answer can, of course, be found by rearranging the PVA formula and solving for the amount of the payment, that procedure is complex and unwieldy in comparison with using a table or financial calculator. Hence only the latter two methods will be explained here.

Using the Table

In order to use the table, simply divide the original loan balance by the PVA factor for the proper i and n. When calculating the PVA, you *multiplied* the proper factor by one of the payments. When calculating the amount of one of the payments, you should *divide* the PVA by the proper factor.

Since in the present illustration the loan payments are to be made at the end of each year, you can use the PVA factor for 15 years and 11% shown in table A.4. Dividing this factor, 7.1909, into the $50,000 loan amount produces the size of the annual payment, $6,953.23. (Note, by the way, the amount of interest that will be paid on this loan. The total to be repaid will be $104,298.45, that is, 15 x $6,953.23. Since the loan principal is $50,000, the interest is $54,298.45.)

If the terms of the loan, on the other hand, had called for the first annual installment payment to be made immediately, it would be necessary first to convert the PVA factor for 15 years and 11% into a PVAD factor. This would be accomplished by multiplying 7.1909 by 1.11. The resulting PVAD factor, 7.9819, would then be divided into the $50,000 loan amount to produce the annual payment of $6,264.17. The total amount of interest to be paid in this situation would be $43,962.55, that is, ($6,264.17 x 15) − $50,000.

Using the HP-12C or BA-II

Using a financial calculator is even more efficient, as well as being more precise than the table because of a lesser problem of rounding. To illustrate, assume that in a negligence case a jury has awarded $125,000 to be used to support an injured child until he or she reaches age 21, 11 years from now. How much will this capital sum and interest earnings thereon provide for the child per year if the fund earns 8 percent compound interest?

On the HP-12C, depress the following keys: 125000, CHS, PV, 8, i, 11, n, blue g, BEG (or END, depending on when the first withdrawal will be made), and PMT. The payment under the beginning-of-year assumption is $16,212.54. Under the end-of-year assumption it is $17,509.54. On the BA-II the same answers are found by pressing 125000, PV, 8, %i, 11, N, DUE (or 2nd, depending on when the first withdrawal will be made), and PMT.

Variations from the foregoing debt service and capital liquidation problems are problems in which the task is to compute n, the number of installment payments that will be required or possible, or i, the interest rate being charged or needed. For such purposes a financial calculator is the most effective tool.

Assume, for example, that a company plans to borrow $200,000 to expand its fleet of delivery vehicles. If the financial officer believes the company can afford to make loan repayments of $55,000 per year beginning a year from now, and if the lending institution is quoting an interest rate of 10.5 percent, how long will it take to repay the loan? On the BA-II press the following keys: 200000, PV, 55000, PMT, 10.5, %i, 2nd, and N. The answer is 4.8172 years.[3]

On the other hand, if the financial officer believes the company must have the loan repaid in 4 years, what interest rate must he or she obtain from the lending institution to accomplish this objective? On the HP-12C, press 200000, CHS, PV, 55000, PMT, 4, n, blue g, END, and i. The answer, an unlikely 3.9245 percent, will eventually appear on the screen. Even if the borrower and lender use the BA-II, they are unlikely to reach agreement on an acceptable interest rate. Press 200000, PV, 55000, PMT, 4, N, 2nd, and %i. After a brief delay, the 3.9245 percent rate is again displayed.

Creating an Amortization Schedule

Another useful calculation in connection with debt service problems is to generate an amortization schedule. In any installment loan, a portion of each payment is used to pay interest and the rest is applied to reduce the principal of the loan. Over the term of the loan the interest portion of the payment falls and the principal portion rises. The amortization schedule enables you to see, year by year, how much is being applied toward each.

To illustrate, assume a $1,000 loan with a compound annual interest rate of 11 percent is to be repaid in four equal annual installments beginning in one year. The amount of each payment is $322.33. How much of each year's payment will be applied to interest and how much to principal?[4]

If you are preparing the amortization schedule manually, you should set up a worksheet with column headings as shown in the following table.

TABLE 5.2
Sample Loan Amortization Schedule

	(1)	(2)	(3)	(4)	(5)
Year	Unpaid Balance, Beginning of Year	Payment, End of Year	Interest Payment i x (1)	Principal Payment (2) − (3)	Unpaid Balance, End of Year (1) − (4)
1	$1,000.00	$322.33	$110.00	$212.33	$787.67
2	787.67	322.33	86.64	235.69	551.98
3	551.98	322.33	60.72	261.61	290.37
4	290.37	322.33	31.94	290.39	(.02)

After inserting the initial loan amount and the first year's payment, calculate the first year's interest by multiplying the 11 percent interest rate by the loan amount. This produces the figure for column (3). The balance of the payment, shown in column (4), is principal and is subtracted from the initial loan amount to produce the unpaid balance at the end of the first year, as shown in column (5). This amount is also the unpaid balance at the beginning of the second year, as shown in column (1). Again, 11 percent of this amount is the second year's interest in column (3), the remainder of the payment goes on principal in column (4), and so on through the end of the fourth and final year of the loan.

If you are using the HP-12C to create an amortization schedule, note that the n key also contains a yellow AMORT (amortization) function. Note also the $x \gtrless y$ key in the second row of the keyboard. Both of these will be used to solve the problem.

First enter the basic data about the problem in this illustration. Press 11, i, blue g, END, 1000, PV, 322.33, CHS, and PMT. Now press 1 (because one payment will be made per year), yellow f, and AMORT. The amount displayed, $110.00, is the first year's interest. Next press the $x \gtrless y$ key to see the principal payment, $212.33. Then press RCL and PV to show the unpaid balance at the end of year one, $787.67. Repeat the sequence as shown below to see the amounts in the following years.

Year	Keystrokes	Interest	Keystroke	Principal	Keystroke	Unpaid Balance
2	1, yellow f, AMORT	$86.64	$x \gtrless y$	$235.69	RCL, PV	$551.98
3	1, yellow f, AMORT	$60.72	$x \gtrless y$	$261.61	RCL, PV	$290.37
4	1, yellow f, AMORT	$31.94	$x \gtrless y$	$290.39	RCL, PV	($ .02)

The total interest paid during the 4 years is, thus, ($110.00 + $86.64 + $60.72 + $31.94=) $289.30. The principal repaid, of course, totals (except for $.02 due to rounding) $1,000.

The procedure for creating an amortization schedule on the BA-II calculator is slightly different from that for the HP-12C. Note the key marked $x \gtrless y$ in the third row from the top in the left column. Note also that this key has a second function, P/I, (for Principal/Interest) printed above it. Both functions of this key will be used to create the amortization schedule.

First, however, enter the basic data about the problem in this illustration. Press the following keys: 1000, PV, 4, N, 11, %i, 322.33, and PMT. Now press 1 (for the first payment), 2nd, and P/I and the first year's principal payment is displayed, $212.33. Press $x \gtrless y$ and the interest, $110.00, is displayed. To find the second year's principal payment press 2, 2nd, P/I, and $235.68 is displayed. The second year's interest, $86.65, is found by pressing the $x \gtrless y$ key. For the third year press 3, 2nd, P/I (the principal payment is $261.61) and $x \gtrless y$ (the interest is $60.72). Finally, for the fourth year press 4, 2nd, P/I ($290.39 is the principal payment) and $x \gtrless y$ ($31.94 is the interest). The interest payments total ($110.00 + $86.65 + $60.72 + $31.94=) $289.31. The principal repaid is, of course, (except for $.01 due to rounding) $1,000.

NOTES

1. See Chapter 4 for an explanation of the terms "annuity" and "annuity due."

2. In reality most installment loans call for monthly payments. In this chapter, however, it will be assumed that the periodic loan payments are made annually. The method for computing monthly payments will be explained in Chapter 8.

3. As was explained in Chapter 2, the HP-12C is considerably less precise than the BA-II in solving for n. In this case, the HP-12C would give an answer of 5 years.

4. The procedure for creating an amortization schedule where the loan is repaid through monthly installment payments is the same as described in this section except that (a) the figure used as the periodic payment should be the monthly payment; (b) the figure used as the interest rate should be the annual rate divided by 12; and (c) the number used as the n should be the total number of monthly payments to be made. See the discussion of simple annuities in Chapter 8.

PROBLEMS

1. You have leased the office building you own to a company that pays you $25,000 as rent each year. The next rental payment is due in one year.

    (a) For what lump sum amount would you sell the next three payments today if you could invest the proceeds at a 12.5 percent compound annual rate of return?

    (b) For what amount would you sell them if the next rental payment is due later today?

2. Which would you prefer to have: $10,000 today in a lump sum or $1,000 per year for 13 years, beginning one year from now, if interest rates are

    (a) 4 percent?

    (b) 6 percent?

3. A bank is willing to lend you $15,000 to make some home improvements. The loan is to be repaid in five equal annual installments, beginning one year from now. If the interest rate on the loan is 10 percent,

    (a) what will be the size of the annual payment?

    (b) how much of the second payment will be interest?

    (c) how much of the final payment will be principal?

4. The account in which you deposited your inheritance has a present balance of $48,000. If the account is credited with 13 percent compound annual interest and if you plan to withdraw from it $7,500 per year beginning now, how long will it be before the balance is zero?

5. Suppose that a bank will lend you $10,000 if you agree to repay $4,199.31 at the end of each of the next 3 years. What compound annual interest rate is the bank charging you?

SOLUTIONS

1. (a) You would be willing to sell the next three payments for about $59,533 today. In table A.4, the PVA factor for 3 years, 12.5% is 2.3813. $25,000 x 2.3813 = $59,532.50. On a financial calculator with $25,000 as the end-of-year PMT, 3 as the n, and 12.5 as the i, PVA = $59,533.61.

   (b) In this case the selling price would be higher, about $66,975. The PVAD factor is 2.3813 x 1.125, or 2.6790. $25,000 x 2.6790 = $66,975.00. If you use a financial calculator, the present value of the three beginning-of-year PMTs is $66,975.31.

2. (a) $10,000 now is preferable. In table A.4 the PVA factor for 4%, 13 years is 9.9856. $1,000 x 9.9856 = $9,985.60 PVA. On the financial calculator, PVA = $9,985.65.

   (b) $10,000 in a lump sum now is even more preferable at the 6 percent discount rate. The PVA factor of 8.8527 multiplied by $1,000 = $8,852.70. On the financial calculator, PVA = $8,852.68.

3. (a) The PVA factor in table A.4 is 3.7908. The payment would be $15,000 ÷ 3.7908, or $3,956.95. On the financial calculator, with $15,000 as the PV, 5 as the n, and 10 as the i, the end-of-year PMT = $3,956.96.

   (b) and (c)
   It is possible, though cumbersome, to create an amortization schedule such as the following without using a financial calculator.

Year	(1) Unpaid Balance, Beginning of Year	(2) Payment, End of Year	(3) Interest Payment 10% x (1)	(4) Principal Payment (2) − (3)	(5) Unpaid Balance, End of Year (1) − (4)
1	$15,000.00	$3,956.95	$1,500.00	$2,456.95	$12,543.05
2	12,543.05	3,956.95	1,254.31	2,702.64	9,840.41
3	9,840.41	3,956.95	984.04	2,972.91	6,867.50
4	6,867.50	3,956.95	686.75	3,270.20	3,597.30
5	3,597.30	3,956.95	359.73	3,597.22	.08

   Thus the interest portion of the second payment will be $1,254.31 and the principal portion of the final payment will be $3,597.22. If you use the much faster financial calculator technique as described in the text with $3,956.96 as the end-of-year PMT, the second interest payment is $1,254.30 and the final principal payment is $3,597.23.

4. First divide $48,000 by the $7,500 payment to produce a PVAD (because the payments are to begin now) factor of 6.400. Then use the 13% column of table A.4 to find the n closest to this factor. The PVA factor for 10 years, multiplied by 1.13, is 6.1316. The PVA factor for 11 years, multiplied by 1.13, is 6.4262. Thus n is between 10 and 11 years, and is closer to 11. By a process of interpolation or by using a financial calculator with $7,500 as the beginning-of-year PMT, you can find the precise n = 10.9058.

5. First divide $10,000 by the $4,199.31 payment to produce a PVA (because the payments are to be made at the end of each year) factor of 2.3813. In the 3-year row of table A.4, this factor appears in the 12.5% column. Alternatively, enter the PV, n, and end-of-year PMT in a financial calculator to find that $i = 12.5000\%$.

CHAPTER 6

DEALING WITH UNEVEN CASH FLOWS

Chapters 4 and 5 contained explanations of how to compute the future value and present value of an annuity (or an annuity due). By definition of the term "annuity", the discussion dealt only with cases in which each of the payments or deposits in the series was of the same amount. The present chapter explains how to compute the future value or present value of a stream of *uneven* payments or deposits. The ability to do so will be useful in and of itself to solve several types of problems. It also is essential in order to evaluate various types of investments through discounted cash flow analysis, as will be explained in Chapter 7. The present chapter begins with an explanation of how to compute the present value of a stream of uneven cash flows and then takes up the calculation of the future value of such flows.

PRESENT VALUE OF UNEVEN CASH FLOWS

Assume that a young man will be entering college in one year. The estimated tuition is $6,000 to be paid at the start of the freshman year, $6,600 at the start of the sophomore year, $7,250 at the start of the junior year, and $8,100 at the start of the senior year. How much should be on hand today in an account earning 8.5 percent interest in order to just meet these four tuition payments as they come due? What is the present value of this series of uneven cash flows discounted at 8.5 percent?

The solution of a simple problem of this sort actually involves no techniques that have not already been covered earlier in this book. All that is needed is to compute the present value of each of the four tuition payments and add them together. In other words, the present value of this stream of uneven payments is simply the sum of the present values of the four single sums.

Using Time Value Tables

Since this sequence of cash flows is fairly brief, simple tools such as a time value formula or a table can be used to compute the present value fairly quickly. Table A.2 in Appendix A will be used here to provide the appropriate 8.5 percent factors needed to solve the problem.

End of Year	Tuition Amount	PVSS Factor	PVSS
1	$6,000	0.9217	$ 5,530.20
2	6,600	0.8495	5,606.70
3	7,250	0.7829	5,676.03
4	8,100	0.7216	5,844.96
Total			$22,657.89

If $22,657.89 is placed on deposit today, and if 8.5 percent compound interest is earned on the account balance over the next four years, there will be just enough to meet each of the estimated tuition payments as they fall due. After the final payment is made, the account balance will be essentially zero. Table 6.1 shows the pattern of the account balance over the four years.

TABLE 6.1
Liquidation of a Capital Sum Compounding at 8.5% Interest
Through Uneven Cash Withdrawals

Year	Beginning Balance	Interest Earnings	Cash Withdrawal	Ending Balance
1	$22,657.89	$1,925.92	$6,000	$18,583.81
2	18,583.81	1,579.62	6,600	13,563.43
3	13,563.43	1,152.89	7,250	7,466.32
4	7,466.32	634.64	8,100	0.96

This case is an illustration of so-called *ungrouped* cash flows, which means that the cash flow sequence includes no consecutive payments of the same amount and arithmetic sign, positive or negative. Each payment, therefore, has to be discounted separately. In some situations, however, there will also be some *grouped* cash flows, that is, some of the consecutive payments will be of the same amount and flow in the same direction, either in or out. In this case a short cut is possible in finding the present value of the cash flow.

A common example of an uneven cash flow where some of the payments can be grouped is a corporate bond. For example, assume that you are considering purchasing a bond that will pay you interest of $90 per year at the end of each of the next 6 years, as well as the $1,000 face amount at the end of the sixth year.[1] If you wish to earn a rate of return of 13 percent on your money, how much would you pay for the bond? That is, what is the present value, discounted at a 13 percent annual interest rate, of this income stream, which is depicted in figure 6.1?

This series of cash flows actually consists of two components: an annuity of $90 per year for 5 years and a single sum of $1,090 at the end of the sixth year (or an annuity of $90 per year for 6 years and a single sum of $1,000 at the end of the sixth year). Hence to compute the present value of the entire sequence it is necessary to (1) compute the present value of the annuity, (2) compute the present value of the single sum, and (3) add the results together.

Again, the sequence of cash flows is rather short and simple in the present illustration, so the solution can be calculated fairly quickly using time value formulas or tables. For example, table A.4 in Appendix A shows a PVA factor of 3.5172 for 5 years and 13%. Multiplied by the $90 annuity payment, this produces a PVA of $316.55. Table A.2 shows a PVSS factor of .4803 for 6 years and 13%. Multiplied by $1,090 it produces a present value of the sixth year cash flow of $523.53. The present value of the total sequence of cash flows, the price you would be willing to pay for the bond, is, thus, ($316.55 + $523.53 =) $840.08.

FIGURE 6.1

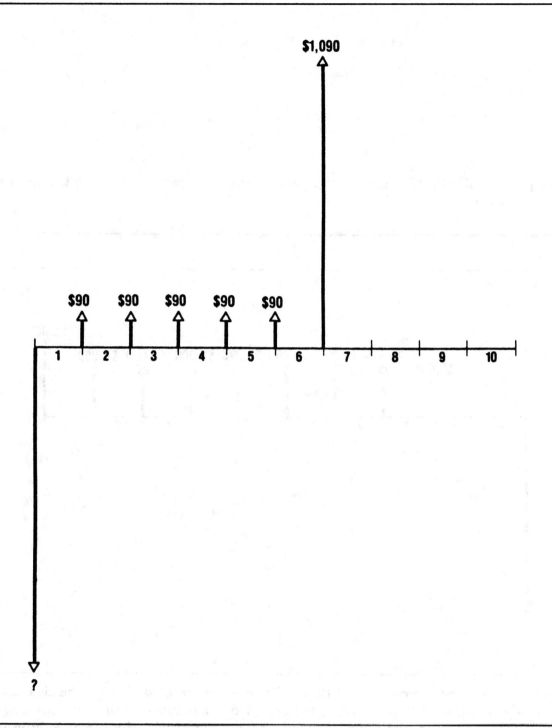

Figure 6.1. *Time Line Depiction of a Bond Value.* The time line depicts the uneven stream of cash flows provided by a bond--5 payments of $90 each and a sixth of $1,090. The problem is to compute the present value of the stream of cash flows.

To take a different situation involving some grouped cash flows, assume you loan a sum of money to a borrower today. The repayment schedule calls for the borrower to make payments to you as follows:

End of Year	Payment Amount
1	$ 0
2	2,000
3-9	3,000
10	5,000

What is the present value of this sequence of payments, which is depicted in figure 6.2, if an 11 percent interest rate is assumed?

FIGURE 6.2

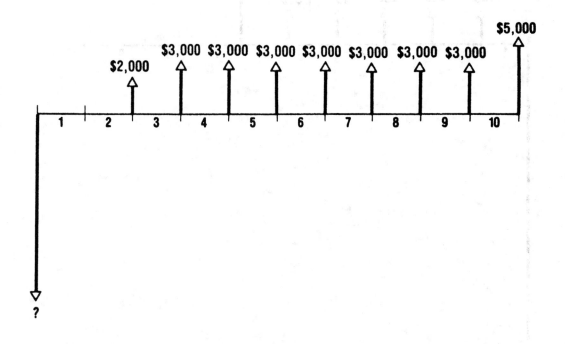

Figure 6.2. *Time Line Depiction of the Present Value of Uneven Cash Flows.* This time line shows a problem in which the task is to compute the present value of a stream of cash flows consisting of zero at the end of year 1, $2,000 at the end of year 2, $3,000 at the end of each of years 3 through 9, and $5,000 at the end of year 10.

The solution to this problem involves several steps. First, the $2,000 payment at the end of year two must be discounted. Second, the present value of a 7-year, $3,000 annuity must be computed. Third, the present value of that annuity must be further discounted as a single sum to compute its present value *today*, rather than its present value 2 years from now when the annuity begins. (Note that this annuity begins at the *start* of the third year, even though the first payment under it is not made until the *end* of the third year.) Fourth, the $5,000 payment at the end of year 10 must be discounted. Finally, the PVSS of the first payment, the twice discounted value of the PVA of the next seven payments, and the PVSS of the ninth payment must be added together to obtain the present value of the entire series of cash flows.

Again you can use tables A.2 and A.4 to solve the problem. From the 11% column find the appropriate factors and apply them as follows:

1. PVSS of payment at end of year 2
   $2,000 x 0.8116 = $ 1,623.20

2. PVA of payments at end of years 3-9
   $3,000 x 4.7122 = $14,136.60

3. PVSS of PVA of payments at end of years 3-9
   $14,136.60 x 0.8116 =   11,473.26

4. PVSS of payment at end of year 10
   $5,000 x 0.3522 =   1,761.00

5. Present value of the cash flows $14,857.46

One last point should be made before some slightly more complex cash flow patterns are taken up. In some problems one or more of the cash flow amounts will be negative. For example, assume you own rental property which is expected to generate net income for you of $15,000 per year at the end of each of the next 15 years, except for year 10. In that year you estimate that replacement of the heating and air conditioning units will be necessary, causing a *net cash outflow* for the year of $6,000. What is the present value of this stream of cash flows discounted at 9 percent?

In this case the only difference in procedure for finding the solution is that the present value of the net cash outflow must be *subtracted* from the aggregate present value of the net cash inflows. Specifically, in this illustration,

1. PVA of inflows at end of years 1-9
   $15,000 x 5.9952 $ 89,928.00

2. PVA of inflows at end of years 11-15
   $15,000 x 3.8897 = $58,345.50

3. PVSS of PVA of inflows at end of years 11-15
   $58,345.50 x .4224   24,645.14

4. Present value of cash inflows $114,573.14

5. PVSS of outflow at end of year 10
   $6,000 x .4224   (2,534.40)

6. Present value of the net cash flows $112,038.74

As you can see, the illustrations are becoming a bit complex and the use of tables to solve them is starting to be a little unwieldy. To reduce the difficulty, you may be able to express the cash flows of a problem in slightly different terms that are easier to deal with. For example, the preceding pattern of cash flows could have been expressed as

1. an annuity of $15,000 for 15 years, and

2. an outflow of $21,000 at the end of year 10 (that is, $15,000 that needs to be subtracted out of the annuity and $6,000 that was the actual net outflow).

Calculation of the present value of this pattern of cash flows could have been completed in far fewer steps than were presented above.

Using the BA-II

In all the illustrative problems up to this point, the solution could be found fairly easily because the pattern of payments was short and simple. Tools such as the time value formulas or tables A.2 and A.4 and a simple calculator suffice in such situations for computing and totalling the present value of the individual cash flows or, in the case of groups of level cash flows, the annuities.

Likewise, for problems involving short sequences of uneven cash flows the BA-II financial calculator can be a useful tool with which to calculate the present value. The procedure requires that each cash flow amount, or each group of consecutive cash flows that are of the same amount and arithmetic sign, be entered and discounted separately and then totalled. Technically all of this can be done inside the BA-II calculator itself through a deft use of the store (STO), SUM, and recall (RCL) keys in the left hand column of the keyboard (as explained in Chapter 10 of the BA-II owner's manual.) However, this author has found that approach to be quite complex. Therefore, even though it entails the loss of some "purity", it is suggested that the best approach if you wish to use the BA-II is to supplement the calculator with an old fashioned pencil and paper.

To illustrate the use of the BA-II for calculating the present value of an income stream where uneven cash flows are present, assume an investment involves the following sequence of cash flows.

End of year 1	$5,000	inflow
End of year 2	$3,000	outflow
End of year 3	$4,000	inflow
End of year 4	$6,000	inflow

Calculate the present value at a discount rate of 6 percent.

1. Present value of cash inflows (jot down each one):

   5000, FV, 1, N, 6, %i, 2nd, PV $ 4,716.98 (ON/C)

   4000, FV, 3, N, 6, %i, 2nd, PV   3,358.48 (ON/C)

   6000, FV, 4, N, 6, %i, 2nd, PV   4,752.56 (ON/C)

   Total (manually or on the calculator) $12,828.02 (ON/C)

2. Present value of cash outflow

     3000, FV, 2, N, 6, %i, 2nd, PV   (2,669.99) (ON/C)

3. Present value of the net cash flows $10,158.03

As you can imagine, if a problem entails a lengthy sequence of cash flows of uneven amounts, the BA-II becomes an impractical tool to use in this fashion. Then the HP-12C or a computer will be a far superior device. (Perhaps this is one of the reasons that HP-12Cs and computers typically cost more than BA-IIs.)

Using the HP-12C

Often a lengthy series of cash flows is involved in a problem. Also, frequently the series will involve many different payment amounts, some years of zero flows, and perhaps even some changes of arithmetic signs from positive to negative net flows and back again. For most such cases, the HP-12C calculator is very well suited. For problems that exceed the usually ample capacity of the HP-12C, a computer program may be needed.

Ungrouped Cash Flows at End of Year. First to be explained will be the use of the HP-12C to solve problems in which there are no consecutive cash flows that are of the same amount. In this case the HP-12C has the capacity to solve problems involving up to 20 cash flows that occur at the end of each year (or 21 that occur at the beginning of each year).

To illustrate, assume an investment will produce the following pattern of net cash inflows during the next 20 years.

End of Year	Cash Flow	End of Year	Cash Flow
1	$ 500	11	$ 0
2	1,100	12	2,150
3	1,150	13	2,250
4	1,175	14	2,350
5	1,000	15	2,450
6	2,600	16	2,600
7	2,700	17	650
8	2,800	18	2,700
9	2,900	19	2,800
10	1,000	20	2,900

This set of data, together with the discount rate to be used, represents the maximum capacity that the HP-12C can handle, and then only if the calculator's memory is completely empty of other information.[2] As will be explained below, the calculator's capacity can be expanded if some of the data consist of grouped data, that is, consecutive equal amounts with the same arithmetic sign, either plus or minus (for example, if each of the last three cash flows shown above were $2,800). Note in this problem, by the way, that some of the cash flows are of equal amounts (years six and 16, years seven and 18, years eight and 19, and years nine and 20). Nevertheless, these are not grouped data because the equal amounts do not occur in consecutive years.

To solve a present value problem on the HP-12C where the cash flows are ungrouped and begin one or more periods in the future, first look at the PMT key in the top row of the keyboard. Note that it also contains a blue CFj function. (The CFj symbol stands for juxtaposed, or side-by-side, cash flows.) This function, will be used to enter the amount of each cash flow, including zero amounts. After all the payments in the series are entered, the discount rate will be entered with the i key as usual. Finally, note that the PV key in the top row of the keyboard also contains a yellow function, NPV, net present value. The yellow f key and NPV will be used to produce the solution.

To illustrate the process, assume that you have a deferred compensation agreement with your employer. Under the agreement the employer is obligated to pay you the following amounts:

End of year 1	$ 0
End of year 2	$75,000
End of year 3	$80,000
End of year 4	$85,000
End of year 5	$90,000

If you use a discount rate of 12.5 percent, what is the present value of this future income stream? Press 0, blue g, and CFj. The initial year's zero value has now been entered. Press 75000, blue g, and CFj to reflect the amount to be received at the end of year two. Press 80000, blue g, and CFj to enter the cash inflow at the end of year three. Enter the remaining two payments by pressing 85000, blue g, CFj, 90000, blue g, and CFj. Now enter the discount rate by pressing 12.5 and the i key. Finally, compute the present value of the income stream by pressing the yellow f key and NPV. The answer, $218,454.50, appears on the display.

Now you should test your skills a bit further by solving the preceding lengthy problem containing 20 cash flows. Hopefully you will conclude that, if you use an 8 percent interest rate, the present value of this income stream is $16,638.51. (Did you remember to enter the zero amount in year 11?) If you would like to recalculate the present value of this income stream at a discount rate of, for example, 7.5 percent, simply press 7.5, i, yellow f, and NPV. The revised amount, $17,395.56, is displayed.

Grouped Cash Flows at End of Year. The HP-12C can solve present value problems involving more than 20 cash flows if the series includes some grouped data. It has sufficient capacity to deal with up to 20 cash flow *amounts* (in addition to a cash flow at the beginning of the first year or a series of grouped cash flows that start at the beginning of the first year). A total of 20 cash flow amounts may entail more than 20 cash flows, since grouped data count as only one cash flow amount in the HP-12C. For example, a cash flow of $50,000 followed by 40 annual cash flows of $2,000 involves 41 cash flows but only two cash flow amounts, well within the capacity of the HP-12C. For problems that include grouped data you should enter, along with the amount of each such cash flow, the total number of times it occurs in succession, including the first time. This number is entered by means of the blue Nj function on the FV key in the center of the top row of the keyboard. Up to 99 consecutive flows of a given amount can be entered into the machine in this manner.

To illustrate the process, assume that you are considering investing in a "great opportunity" that will yield a cash inflow to you starting next year of $6,000 per year for 5 years, followed by $4,000 per year for 10 years, followed by $2,000 per year for 15 years, followed by a lump sum payment of $25,000. Compute the present value of this income stream utilizing an 8 percent discount rate.

Begin by entering the amount of the initial inflow: 6000, blue g, and CFj. Since it will occur a total of five times (including the first), press 5, blue g, and Nj. Now enter the next group of inflows: 4000, blue g, CFj; and the number of times this amount will occur: 10, blue g, Nj. Enter the third group of inflows by pressing 2000, blue g, CFj, 15, blue g, and Nj. Then enter the 31st and final inflow, 25000, blue g, CFj. Finally, enter the interest rate by pressing 8 and i. Compute the answer by pressing yellow f and NPV and the answer, $49,920.35, appears on the screen. You can revise the interest rate if you wish simply by entering the new rate and pressing i, yellow f, and NPV.

Cash Flows at Beginning of Year. Each of the preceding illustrations of how to use the HP-12C involved cash flows that occurred at the end of the year. If the cash flows occur at the beginning of the year, only a slight change in procedure is needed to find the present value of the payment stream. Take another look at the PV key, and note that it has a blue CFo function. If the problem to be solved entails cash flows at the beginning of each year, the first such flow (or group of consecutive cash inflows or outflows of equal amount) is entered by means of this blue CFo function. (The symbol CFo stands for original cash flow.) Subsequent cash flows are then entered via the CFj function in the manner described above.[3]

To illustrate, if a 12 percent discount rate is used, what is the present value of the following series of cash flows?

Beginning of Year	Amount
1-5	$3,500
6-10	2,500
11	1,500
12	500

To compute the present value of the first five cash flows, press 3500, blue g, *CFo*, 5, blue g, and Nj. The next five cash flows are entered by pressing 2500, blue g, CFj, 5, blue g, and Nj. The last two cash flows are entered by pressing 1500, blue g, CFj, 500, blue g, and CFj. The solution is found by entering the discount rate (12 and i) and pressing yellow f and NPV. The answer, $20,484.67, appears on the display.

Payments Growing by a Constant Percentage

In many cases time value of money problems involve the need to discount to their present value a stream of payments that grow by a constant annual percentage. Adjusting for an assumed inflation rate is often the underlying motivation.

For example, assume that you wish to have an income stream of $25,000 per year *in constant purchasing power* for each of the next 10 years, starting immediately. How large a capital sum would you need to set aside today to meet this objective if the annual inflation rate is assumed to be 5 percent and if the principal sum to be liquidated can be assumed to produce a rate of return of 8 percent per year? What is the present value, discounted at 8 percent, of this 10-year stream of payments that will rise by 5 percent per year?

You could, of course, calculate the amount of each of the 10 payments, discount each of them for the appropriate number of years, and add up the results. There is, however, a better way to produce the answer to this problem. If done manually, it involves using the following formula:

$$PV = (1 + i) \left[\frac{1 - \left[\frac{(1 + \text{growth rate})}{(1 + i)} \right]^n}{(i - \text{growth rate})} \right] \times \text{amount of 1st payment}$$

In the present illustration, the answer is

$$= 1.08 \times \left[\frac{1 - \left[\frac{1.05}{1.08} \right]^{10}}{(.08 - .05)} \right] \times \$25,000$$

$$= 1.08 \times \left[\frac{1 - .7545}{.03} \right] \times \$25,000$$

$$= 1.08 \times \quad 8.1836 \quad \times \$25,000$$

$$= \$220,957.20$$

If the first $25,000 payment is to be made after one year, rather than immediately, the answer found through this formula should be divided by $(1 + i)$. In this case the present value would be ($220,957.20 ÷ 1.08 =) $204,590.00.

Rather than laboring through the formula, you may prefer to use the HP-12C or BA-II calculator to solve this type of problem. On the HP-12C, the keystrokes would be as follows for the beginning-of-year approach:

blue g, BEG, 25000, PMT,	(to enter the first payment)
1.08, ENTER, 1.05, ÷, 1, −, 100, x, i,	(to enter the adjusted discount rate)
10, n, PV	(to enter the n and produce the solution)

The answer, $220,955.95, will appear on the display. Dividing this result by 1.08 will produce the end-of-year solution, $204,588.84.

On the BA-II, the keystrokes for the beginning-of-year solution would be as follows:

25000, PMT,	(to enter the first payment)
1.08, ÷, 1.05, −, 1, x, 100, =, %i,	(to enter the adjusted discount rate)
10, N, DUE, PV	(to enter the n and produce the solution)

The answer, $220,955.95, will appear on the display. Dividing this result by 1.08 will produce the end-of-year solution, $204,588.84.

FUTURE VALUE OF UNEVEN CASH FLOWS

The following pages deal with the reverse of the previous set of problems and explain how to calculate the future value of a series of uneven cash flows. The explanation can be brief because the approach to solving such problems parallels that for solving present value problems.

Assume that a business plans to make the following series of contributions to fund certain obligations under its pension plan:

End of Year	Amount
1	$30,000
2	40,000
3-5	50,000
6-10	60,000

If these contributions are credited with 10 percent interest per year, how much will be in the fund at the end of the 10th year? What is the future value of this series of uneven cash flows?

The solution of this type of problem entails compounding each payment from the time it is made until the end of the tenth year and totalling the results. Thus the first $30,000 should be compounded for 9 years at 10 percent to produce its FVSS. The second should be compounded for 8 years, the third for 7 years, etc. The final $60,000 payment, of course, earns no interest because it is made at the end of the 10th year.

Using Time Value Tables

If, as in the present illustration, the sequence of cash flows is brief and straightforward, the basic future value formulas or tables can be used to produce a solution. For example, table A.1 can provide the nine FVSS factors to be applied to the various payments. Alternatively, since this illustrative problem includes two sets of grouped data ($50,000 per year for 3 years and $60,000 per year for 5 years), table A.3 can be used to provide FVA factors. It must be remembered, however, that the FVA of the three payments at the end of years three, four, and five must be further compounded by means of an FVSS factor to produce the future value of these three contributions as of the end of the 10th year.

Specifically, then, the future value of this series of uneven cash flows at 10 percent can be found as shown below.[4]

1. FVSS of payment at end of year 1
   $30,000 x 2.3579 $ 70,737.00

2. FVSS of payment at end of year 2
   $40,000 x 2.1436   85,744.00

3. FVA of payments at end of years 3-5
   $50,000 x 3.3100 = $165,500

4. FVSS of FVA of payments at end of years 3-5
   $165,500 x 1.6105   266,537.75

5. FVA of payments at end of years 6-10
   $60,000 x 6.1051   366,306.00

6. Future value of the cash flows $789,324.75

Using the BA-II

As is true in the solution of present value problems explained earlier in this chapter, the BA-II financial calculator also can be used to find the future value of a series of uneven payments. Again, however, to this author a bit of pencil and paper work seems to be a helpful supplement to the machine.

To illustrate the approach, compute the future value at the end of the sixth year of the following sequence of payments at an interest rate of 15.2 percent. (Note that in this illustration the cash flows occur at the beginning of each year.)

Beginning of Year	Amount
1	$500
2-5	300
6	200

1. Future value of payment in year 1
   (jot it down):
   500, PV, 15.2, %i, 6, N, 2nd, FV $1,168.65 (ON/C)

2. Future value of payments in years 2-5
   as of end of year 5 (jot it down):
   300, PMT, 15.2, %i, 4, N, DUE, FV
   $1,730.74 (2nd, CMR)

3. Future value of payments in years 2-5
   as of end of year 6 (jot it down):
   1730.74, PV, 15.2, %i, 1, N, 2nd, FV $1,993.81 (ON/C)

4. Future value of payment in year 6
   (jot it down):
   200, PV, 15.2, %i, 1, N, 2nd, FV $ 230.40 (ON/C)

5. Total (manually or on calculator) $3,392.86

Using the HP-12C

Like the BA-II, the HP-12C is not constructed to calculate *directly* the future value of a series of uneven cash flows. Therefore it can be used in the same fashion as the BA-II in the preceding illustration, with the help of a "cheat sheet" if desired, or with the help of the store (STO) and recall (RCL) functions if you are a purist.

However, there is a more efficient way on the HP-12C. Since the HP-12C does have the capability to compute the *present* value of a series of uneven cash flows, as was explained earlier in this chapter, you can compute the single sum which is the present value of the cash flows and then compute the future value of that single sum. This provides the same result as if you calculated the future value of the cash flows directly.

For example, assume the following sequence of cash flows:

End of Year	Amount
1	$500
2-5	600
6-8	700

Calculate the future value as of the end of year eight using a 7 percent interest rate.

Begin by computing the present value of these cash flows as explained earlier in this chapter. Press the keys as shown below.

500, blue g, CFj
600, blue g, CFj, 4, blue g, Nj
700, blue g, CFj, 3, blue g, Nj
7, i, yellow f, NPV

The present value, $3,676.43, appears on the display. Now carry this present value forward as a single sum to the end of year eight using the same 7 percent interest rate by pressing the following keys:

ENTER, CHS, PV, 8, n, 7, i, FV

The future value of this series of uneven cash flows, $6,316.79, appears on the display.

Deposits Growing by a Constant Percentage

Now instead of dealing with cash flows that change in an irregular manner we will take up the case of cash flows whose amounts increase each year by a constant percentage. This type of problem frequently arises where someone sets up a savings plan for the attainment of a financial goal and where the amount to be saved each year rises at the same rate as the person's income is expected to grow.

For example, assume that you plan to begin a program of annual saving, beginning with a $500 deposit now. Assume also that you expect your income and, hence, the amount you can save to rise by about 10 percent per year. If your savings generate a 7 percent annual rate of return, how much will be in your account at the end of 5 years? What is the future value, compounded at 7 percent interest, of this 5-year stream of deposits that will rise by 10 percent per year?

You could, of course, calculate the amount of each of the five deposits, compound each of them for the appropriate number of years, and add up the results. There is, however, a faster way. This type of problem can be solved through the use of the following formula where the first deposit is made immediately.

$$FV = (1 + i) \left[\frac{(1 + i)^n - (1 + \text{growth rate})^n}{(i - \text{growth rate})} \right] \times \text{amount of 1st deposit}$$

In the present example, the answer is

$$= (1.07) \left[\frac{(1.07)^5 - (1.10)^5}{(.07 - .10)} \right] \times \$500$$

$$= (1.07) \left[\frac{1.4026 - 1.6105}{-.03} \right] \times \$500$$

$$= 1.07 \times 6.9300 \times \$500$$

$$= \$3,707.55$$

If the first $500 deposit is to be made after one year, rather than immediately, the answer found through this formula should be divided by (1 + i). In this case the future value would be ($3,707.55 ÷ 1.07 =) $3,465.00.

If instead of using the formula you prefer a financial calculator for solving this type of problem, the HP-12C can be used. However, it can compute the solution only in the indirect manner described earlier in this chapter for calculating the future value of uneven cash flows. First compute the present value, and then carry this amount forward as a single sum to the end of the compounding period. The keystrokes needed to solve the present problem, based on the beginning-of-year approach, are as follows:

blue g, BEG, 500, PMT,	(to enter the first deposit)
1.07, ENTER, 1.10, ÷, 1, −, 100, x, i,	(to enter the adjusted discount rate)
5, n, PV,	(to enter the n and produce the present value)
STO, 1, yellow f, FIN,	(to preserve the present value while clearing out the financial registers)
RCL, 1, PV, 7, i, 5, n, FV	(to produce the solution)

The answer, $3,708.59, will appear on the display. Dividing the result by 1.07 will produce the end-of-year solution, $3,465.97.

The BA-II can also be used to solve this type of future value problem. As with the HP-12C, the procedure involves first calculating the present value of the uneven cash flows and then carrying that amount forward as a single sum to the end of the compounding period. The keystrokes needed to solve the present problem, based on the beginning-of-year approach, are as follows:

500, PMT,	(to enter the first deposit)
1.07, ÷, 1.10, −, 1, x, 100, = %i,	(to enter the adjusted discount rate)
5, N, DUE, PV,	(to enter the n and produce the present value)
STO, 2nd, CMR,	(to preserve the present value while clearing out the financial registers)
RCL, PV, 7, %i, 5, N, 2nd, FV	(to produce the solution)

The answer, $3,708.59, will appear on the display. Dividing this result by 1.07 will produce the end-of-year solution, $3,465.97.

NOTES

1. Most corporate bonds pay interest semiannually. For purposes of simplicity, however, annual payments will be assumed here. Chapter 8 deals with compounding and discounting where cash flows occur more frequently than once per year.

2. You may determine the available capacity of the machine for handling data in a problem by pressing the blue g key and the MEM function on the 9 key in the upper right hand section of the keyboard. The number on the right hand side of the display screen is the maximum number of cash flow amounts (in addition to an initial cash outflow in investment problems discussed in the next chapter) that can be processed by the calculator.

3. Alternatively, you could compute the present value under the end-of-year approach described above and multiply the result by $(1 + i)$.

4. You may have noticed that this cash flow can be restated in terms that are easier to handle if you are using tables.

   $30,000 for 10 years
   +$10,000 for 9 years
   +$10,000 for 8 years
   +$10,000 for 5 years

   Compute the future value of each annuity and add them together.

PROBLEMS

1. The divorce is final and you have been awarded the following alimony: $5,000 at the end of each of the next 3 years, plus $6,000 at the end of each of the following 5 years, plus $7,000 at the end of each of the following 10 years. If you remarry, however, you receive no further alimony. Measured in terms of present value and a discount rate of 6.5 percent, what will your wedding cost if you remarry today?

2. To convince yourself of the wisdom of your recent decision to quit smoking (and this time you really mean it), you plan at the end of each of the next 5 years to put into a savings account earning 6 percent compound annual interest the money you would have spent on cigarettes. You anticipate that the amounts of the five deposits will be $400, $450, $500, $550, and $600. If all goes according to plan, how much will be in your account after 5 years?

3. Which of the following income streams would you rather have if interest rates currently are 7 percent?

Beginning of Year	Cash Flow		End of Year	Cash Flow
1	$2,000		1	0
2	$2,500		2	0
3	$3,000	OR	3	$5,500
4	$3,000		4	$5,500
5	$3,000		5	$5,500

4. Your race horse is a sure thing to win $60,000 for you at the end of each of the next 3 years, after which you believe that the horse will be able to earn about $10,000 per year in stud fees at the end of each of 5 years. If you insist on a compound annual rate of return of at least 20 percent, what would you accept for the horse today?

5. Tuition at the university your daughter will be attending next year is expected to be $11,000 at that time and to rise by about 8 percent per year thereafter. You plan to set aside today a capital sum that, invested at 6 percent interest, will be just sufficient to pay her tuition in full at the start of each of the 4 years. How large a capital sum will be needed to accomplish this objective?

6. Your goal is to have accumulated a capital sum of $75,000 when you retire 12 years from now. You plan to make an initial deposit of $2,000 today, and on each of the following 11 annual anniversary dates you will deposit an amount that is 10 percent higher than the previous year's deposit. If your deposits earn 7 percent interest per year, will you reach your goal?

SOLUTIONS

1. Not counting the cost of the gown, the organist, the flowers, the photographer, etc., the wedding will cost you $64,287.34 in lost alimony, computed as shown below, using factors in tables A.2 and A.4.

The present value of the first series of payments is $13,242.50.	($5,000 x 2.6485 = $13,242.50)
The present value of the second series of payments as of the beginning of year 4 is $24,934.20.	($6,000 x 4.1557 = $24,934.20)
The present value of this amount as of the beginning of year one is $20,640.53.	($24,934.20 x .8278 = $20,640.53)
The present value of the third series of payments as of the beginning of year 9 is $50,321.60.	($7,000 x 7.1888 = $50,321.60)
The present value of this amount as of the beginning of year one is $30,404.31.	($50,321.60 x .6042 = $30,404.31)
The total present value of the three series of payments is $64,287.34.	($13,242.50 + $20,640.53 + $30,404.31 = $64,287.34)

If you had used a financial calculator such as the HP-12C, including the blue CFj and Nj functions, the present value of these uneven cash flows would be $64,290.04.

2. The future value of these five items of ungrouped data, based on FVSS factors in table A.1, will be as follows:

$400 x 1.2625 = $ 505.00
$450 x 1.1910 = 535.95
$500 x 1.1236 = 561.80
$550 x 1.0600 = 583.00
$600 x 1.0000 = 600.00
Total future value $2,785.75

Use of a financial calculator in the way described in this chapter would produce a future value of the same amount.

3. Using PVSS and PVA factors from tables A.2 and A.4, you can compute the present value of the income stream on the left as $11,694.02.

$2,000 x 1.0000 = $2,000.00
2,500 x .9346 = 2,336.50
$3,000 x 2.6243 x 1.07 x .8734 = 7,357.52

Total present value $11,694.02

The present value of the income stream on the right is higher, $12,606.35.

$$\$5,500 \times 2.6243 \times .8734 = \$12,606.35$$

If you use a financial calculator such as the HP-12C, including the blue CFo, CFj, and Nj functions, the income stream on the left is worth $11,694.34 and that on the right is worth $12,606.99.

4. Based on the appropriate PVA and PVSS factors from tables A.2 and A.4, the horse's present value is

$$
\begin{array}{rl}
\$60,000 \times 2.1065 = & \$126,390.00 \\
\$10,000 \times 2.9906 \times .5787 = & \underline{17,306.60} \\
\text{Total present value} & \$143,696.60
\end{array}
$$

This would be your minimum selling price. (If you use the blue CFj and Nj functions on the HP-12C, the answer is $143,695.67.)

5. The answer may be found through the formula for calculating the present value of a series of payments that grow by a constant percentage. Specifically,

$$PV = (1.06) \left[\frac{1 - \left[\frac{1.08}{1.06}\right]^4}{(.06 - .08)} \right] \times \$11,000$$

$$= (1.06) \left[\frac{1 - 1.0776}{-.02} \right] \times \$11,000$$

$$= 1.06 \times 3.8817 \times \$11,000$$

$$= \$45,260.62$$

But since the first payment is not due for one year, this result should be divided by 1.06 to produce the answer, $42,698.70. Or if you follow the sequence of keystrokes presented in that section of the chapter for the HP-12C or the BA-II, the answer that appears on the display will be $45,261.02. Dividing this by 1.06 produces the answer, $42,699.08.

6. You will not reach the $75,000 goal with the planned funding pattern. The answer may be found through the formula for calculating the future value of a series of deposits that grow by a constant percentage and that begin immediately. Specifically,

$$FV = (1.07) \left[\frac{(1.07)^{12} - (1.10)^{12}}{(.07) - .10)} \right] \times \$2,000$$

$$= (1.07) \left[\frac{2.2522 - 3.1384}{-.03} \right] \times \$2,000$$

$$= 1.07 \times 29.5400 \times \$2,000$$

$$= \$63,215.60$$

Or if you follow the sequence of keystrokes presented in that section of the chapter for the HP-12C or BA-II, the answer that appears on the display will be $63,218.22.

CHAPTER 7

EVALUATING AN INVESTMENT THROUGH DISCOUNTED CASH FLOW ANALYSIS

INTRODUCTION

One of the most common personal and business applications of time value of money principles and techniques is the evaluation of a proposed investment. For example, assume that you are considering the purchase of a bond which will involve a cash outlay now (the purchase price) and a series of cash inflows over several time periods in the future (the interest payments and the face amount). Or perhaps you are considering construction of an apartment building which will involve a cash outlay now and perhaps again next year (the construction costs), after which you anticipate a series of cash inflows for a period of years (the rental payments). Or perhaps the investment under consideration is the purchase (cash outflow) of a piece of equipment which will reduce expenses (cash "inflow") over some future time period.

In all of these types of situations there is a tradeoff: one or more cash outflows in return for one or more cash inflows. The question: are the inflows to be received worth the outflows that will be expended? Is it a good investment? By this point you surely understand that the question cannot be adequately answered without taking into account the time value of money. Discounted cash flow analysis assists you to evaluate an investment by making comparable the time value of the cash outflows and the time value of the cash inflows. It thus can be used to assist in deciding (a) whether or not a proposed investment project is an acceptable one, and (b) how to rank several competing investment opportunities in terms of their relative acceptability.

Of course there is more to evaluating an investment than simply crunching some numbers through various time value of money formulas, tables, or calculator functions. The degree of certainty or uncertainty associated with the various cash outflows and inflows, both in amount, timing, and duration, as well as the tax aspects, also must be considered. Evaluation of the tax elements, is beyond the scope of this book. Risk considerations, however, are incorporated in the interest rate that is used in discounted cash flow analysis.

As you will see, the mechanics of discounted cash flow analysis are quite straightforward when the pattern of the cash outflows and inflows is simple. Life becomes a bit more complex when the amounts of each vary from year to year, and still more complex when the combined effect of the outflows and inflows begins switching from negative to positive to negative to positive, back and forth, from year to year. Some simple situations will be dealt with first, followed gradually by more complicated cases.

DISCOUNTED CASH FLOW TECHNIQUES DEFINED

There are two commonly used techniques for discounted cash flow analysis: calculation of an investment's net present value (NPV) and its internal rate of return (IRR). In addition, there are several variations of the IRR technique, one of which will be discussed later in this chapter.

Net Present Value

The net present value of an investment is defined as the present value of the stream of cash inflows minus the present value of the stream of cash outflows, with both present values calculated on the basis of an appropriate rate of interest. The discount rate used could be one such as the minimum rate of return that is acceptable to the investor in light of his or her assessment of the riskiness of the investment; the cost of capital the investor would have to raise in order to make the investment; or the rate available on another acceptable investment being considered that involves a similar degree of riskiness.

If the result of the NPV calculation is positive, that is, if the present value of the inflow stream exceeds the present value of the outflow stream, the investment is a good one. It provides a net addition to the wealth (in a time value sense) of the investor in the amount of the positive remainder. A positive NPV means that the rate of return provided by the investment (whatever that rate is) exceeds the discount rate being used as the benchmark. If the NPV is negative, the reverse is true and the investment will result in a net reduction in the wealth (in a time value sense) of the investor. And if the NPV is zero, the investment will neither add to nor subtract from the investor's wealth (in a time value sense), so that it is a matter of indifference as to whether the investment should be made.

Internal Rate of Return

The internal rate of return on an investment is the interest rate that equates the present value of the stream of cash inflows to the present value of the stream of cash outflows. If that rate is larger than the minimum rate deemed acceptable by the investor, the investment is a good one and should be pursued. If not, it should be rejected. The criteria for determining the acceptable minimum rate of return are the same as those described in connection with the net present value technique.

Similarity of the NPV and IRR Techniques

Note that these two methods of evaluating an investment are very similar. In computing NPV the investor specifies the minimum acceptable interest rate and determines whether at that rate the present value of the inflows exceeds the present value of the outflows. In computing IRR the investor computes the interest rate that will make the present value of the inflows equal to the present value of the outflows; that is, the investor computes the interest rate that will produce an NPV of zero.

As a general rule, when used to evaluate a particular investment the two techniques will lead the investor to the same conclusion if the same data are used. If the NPV is positive, the IRR normally will be acceptable and the investment will be an attractive one. Conversely, if the NPV is negative, the IRR normally will be unacceptable and the investment should be rejected. When used to *rank* several investments as to their *relative* acceptability, however, there are situations in which the NPV and IRR techniques can produce different results using the same data. In most cases the NPV method is more reliable for purposes of ranking several competing investment possibilities. The project with the largest NPV should be ranked first, the one with the next largest NPV should be ranked second, and so on.

COMPUTING NET PRESENT VALUE: SIMPLE PROBLEMS

Consider the following, very simple investment. You are evaluating the purchase of a piece of equipment that will cost $10,000. It will provide a net cash flow of $4,000 per year at the end of each of the next 4 years, after which it will have no value. If your cost of capital is 10 percent per year, is this a worthwhile investment?[1]

FIGURE 7.1

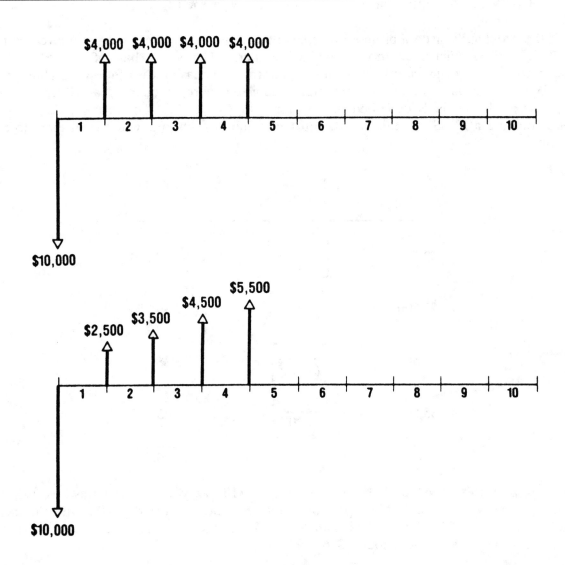

Figure 7.1. *Time Line Representation of NPV Problem: Level and Uneven Inflows.* The upper time line depicts an investment which entails an initial cash outflow of $10,000 and a level stream of four $4,000 cash inflows. In the lower time line the initial cash outflow is the same but the four cash inflows follow an increasing pattern over time.

Depicted on a time line, the cash flows associated with this project appear as shown in the upper half of figure 7.1. The single component of cash outflow, $10,000, occurs immediately, so its present value is $10,000. The four inflows of $4,000 each, totalling $16,000, constitute a 4-year annuity, to be discounted at 10 percent. In Chapter 5 you learned how to calculate a PVA by several methods. For example, using table A.4 in Appendix A you will find the 10%, 4-year PVA factor of 3.1699. Multiplying this by the $4,000 annuity payment produces a PVA of $12,679.60. Subtracting the present value of the outflow, $10,000, you find that the project has a positive NPV of $2,679.60. Your wealth will be increased (in a time value sense) by this amount if you invest in the project. So far, then, calculation of NPV involves little that you have not already learned to do.

And if the problem is made a bit more complex by changing it to one involving uneven cash flows, the calculation still is similar to those explained earlier. The lower half of figure 7.1 shows a modification to the preceding case by including a pattern of increasing cash inflows totalling the same $16,000. The present value of the income stream depicted there, discounted at 10 percent, can be found by one of the methods described in Chapter 3 or Chapter 6. For example, using the basic formula to compute a PVSS you can find the present value of each inflow and total them to produce the solution.

Amount	x $\left[\dfrac{1}{(1 + i)^n}\right]$ =	PVSS
$2,500	$\left[\dfrac{1}{(1.10)}\right]$	$2,272.73
$3,500	$\left[\dfrac{1}{(1.10)^2}\right]$	2,892.56
$4,500	$\left[\dfrac{1}{(1.10)^3}\right]$	3,380.92
$5,500	$\left[\dfrac{1}{(1.10)^4}\right]$	3,756.57
Total		$12,302.78

Subtracting the present value of the outflow stream, $10,000, you find that this investment has a positive net present value of $2,302.78. (It should not be surprising that the NPV with the increasing pattern of cash inflows, $2,302.78, is less than the NPV for the previous case of level cash inflows, $2,679.60, that totalled the same amount, $16,000.)

An additional level of complexity can be introduced into the problem if it is assumed that a *series* of cash outflows is required before the series of cash inflows begins. See, for example, figure 7.2, in which the top time line depicts a project calling for 3 years of uneven cash outflows ($2,000, $1,000, and $500), followed by 5 years of cash inflows ($500, $1,000, $2,000, $2,000, and $3,000). Here the only new procedure is that you must subtract the present value of the *series* of outflows from the present value of the series of inflows. Note also from the time line when the outflows are assumed to occur (at the *beginning* of years one, two, and three) and when the inflows are assumed to occur (at the *end* of years three, four, five, six, and seven).

FIGURE 7.2

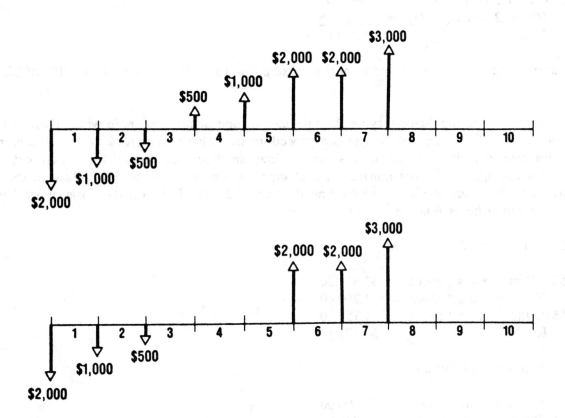

Figure 7.2. *Time Line Representation of NPV Problem: Series of Outflows and Inflows and Years of Zero Outflows or Inflows.* The top line depicts an investment which entails a decreasing series of cash outflows followed by an increasing series of cash inflows. The lower line depicts a similar situation except that there is a gap of 3 years between the last outflow and the first inflow.

Based on the use of table A.2 in Appendix A, the procedure for finding the solution to this problem, with a discount rate of, for example, 8 percent, is as follows:

1. Calculate and sum the present value, discounted at 8 percent, of each of the inflows.

$ 500 in 3 years (.7938) =	$ 396.90
$1,000 in 4 years (.7350) =	735.00
$2,000 in 5 years (.6806) =	1,361.20
$2,000 in 6 years (.6302) =	1,260.40
$3,000 in 7 years (.5835) =	1,750.50
Total	$5,504.00

2. Calculate and sum the present value, discounted at the same rate, of each of the outflows.

        $2,000 in 0 years (1.0000)= $2,000.00
        $1,000 in 1 year   (.9259) =   925.90
        $ 500 in 2 years (.8573) =   428.65
           Total $3,354.55

3. Subtract the result of step two from that of step one to produce the positive NPV of $2,149.45.

One more complicating factor may be the presence of one or more years in which there is no cash outflow or inflow. This does not change the procedure for solving the problem, but it does require a little extra care to make sure the inflows and outflows are being discounted for the correct number of years. For example, if the last illustration is changed so that there is no cash inflow at the end of years three and four (see the bottom time line in figure 7.2), the NPV on the basis of an 8 percent discount rate would be as follows:

1. Present value of inflows

        $2,000 in 5 years (.6806) = $1,361.20
        $2,000 in 6 years (.6302) =   1,260.40
        $3,000 in 7 years (.5835) =   1,750.50
           Total $4,372.10

2. Present value of outflows

        $2,000 in 0 years (1.0000)= $2,000.00
        $1,000 in 1 year   (.9259) =   925.90
        $ 500 in 2 years (.8573) =   428.65
           Total $3,354.55

3. Net present value $1,017.55

The final bit of complexity to be introduced at this point is the presence of one or more cash outflows after the stream of cash inflows has begun. Any inflows and outflows that occur in the same year should be netted against each other. This may produce either of these results: a net cash inflow that is smaller than it otherwise would have been; a net cash inflow that is zero; or a net cash outflow. The first two results involve no new procedures in finding the NPV. The third result does require a little extra work. (As you will see later, this type of result may greatly complicate the task of computing an internal rate of return, however.)

Consider, for example, an investment that calls for the following pattern of cash flows (see figure 7.3):

Beginning of Year	Cash Flow
1	$3,000 outflow
2	$2,000 outflow
3	0
4	$1,000 inflow
5	$2,000 outflow
6	$3,000 inflow
7	$3,000 inflow
8	$3,000 inflow

FIGURE 7.3

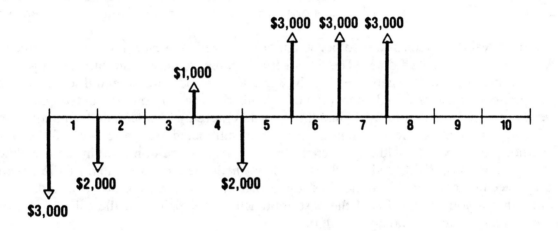

Figure 7.3. *Time Line Representation of NPV Problem: Series of Outflows followed by Year of Zero Flow followed by Series of Inflows Interrupted by Outflow.* This line shows a series of decreasing cash outflows followed by one year in which there is no net inflow or outflow. Thereafter comes one year of a net cash inflow and one of a net cash outflow. Finally, 3 years of level net cash inflows occur.

In this case the only new procedure for solving the problem is that you must remember to add to the present value of the initial outflows in years one and two the present value of the outflow that occurs at the beginning of year five. If, for instance, a 7 percent discount rate is assumed, the present values based on table A.2 in Appendix A are as shown below.

1. Present value of inflows

$1,000 in 3 years (.8163)	=	$ 816.30
$3,000 in 5 years (.7130)	=	2,139.00
$3,000 in 6 years (.6663)	=	1,998.90
$3,000 in 7 years (.6227)	=	1,868.10
Total		$6,822.30

2. Present value of outflows

$3,000 in 0 years (1.0000) = $3,000.00
$2,000 in 1 year (.9346) = 1,869.20
$2,000 in 4 years (.7629) = 1,525.80
   Total $6,395.00

3. Net present value $ 427.30

TOOLS FOR COMPUTING NPV: SIMPLE PROBLEMS

In all the net present value illustrative problems up to this point, the solution could be found fairly easily because the pattern of cash flows was short. As was explained in Chapter 6, tools such as the time value formulas or tables A.2 and A.4 in Appendix A and a simple calculator suffice in such situations for computing and totalling the present value of the individual cash flows or, in the case of a series of level cash flows, the annuity. Likewise, for these problems involving short sequences of inflows or outflows the BA-II financial calculator is a useful tool for calculating net present value.

As net present value problems start to become more involved, however, the use of formulas, tables, or the BA-II starts to be cumbersome. The BA-II, for example, requires that each outflow amount or each group of consecutive outflows that are of the same amount be entered and discounted separately at the appropriate interest rate and then totalled. Similarly, each inflow amount or each group of consecutive inflows that are of the same amount must be entered and discounted separately and then totalled. Finally, the sum of the discounted outflows is subtracted from the sum of the inflows to compute the net present value. Although technically all of this can be done within the calculator itself by using the store (STO), SUM, and recall (RCL) keys in the left hand column of the keyboard, as noted in the preceding chapter this author has found that approach to be quite awkward. Therefore, it is suggested that if you use the BA-II the best approach is to supplement the calculator with pencil and paper notations along the way to a solution.

To illustrate the approach of the BA-II to calculating NPV where uneven cash flows are present, assume an investment project involves the following sequence of cash flows.

Initial investment	$5,250 outflow
End of year 1	$4,500 inflow
End of year 2	$2,500 outflow
End of year 3	$3,500 inflow
End of year 4	$3,000 inflow

Calculate the NPV at a discount rate of 15 percent.

1. Present value of inflows (jot down each one):

4500, FV, 1, N, 15, %i, 2nd, PV	$3,913.04	(ON/C)
3500, FV, 3, N, 15, %i, 2nd, PV	2,301.31	(ON/C)
3000, FV, 4, N, 15, %i, 2nd, PV	1,715.26	(ON/C)
Total (manually or on the calculator)	$7,929.61	(ON/C)

2. Present value of outflows (jot down each one):

Initial investment	$5,250.00
2500, FV, 2, N, 15, %i, 2nd, PV	1,890.36
Total (manually or on the calculator)	$7,140.36 (ON/C)

3. Net present value
   (step 1 minus step 2) $ 789.25

As you can imagine, if an NPV problem entails a lengthy sequence of cash flows of uneven amounts, the BA-II becomes an impractical tool to use. Then the HP-12C or a computer will be a far superior device.

COMPUTING NET PRESENT VALUE: COMPLEX PROBLEMS

For most investment projects that involve a long series of cash outflows or inflows, particularly if they are of uneven amounts, the HP-12C is an excellent tool. Also, the HP-12C can readily handle frequent changes from negative to positive net flows and back again. For NPV problems that exceed the capacity of the HP-12C, a computer program will be needed.

Ungrouped Cash Flows

First to be explained is the use of the HP-12C to solve NPV problems in which there are no consecutive cash flows that are of the same amount and sign. It will be recalled from Chapter 6 that the HP-12C has the capacity to solve problems involving up to 20 cash flow amounts. In addition, it can process the initial cash outflow associated with an investment project. As you will recall from that chapter, the calculator's capacity can be expanded beyond this if some of the data are grouped data.

To solve an NPV problem on the HP-12C where the cash flows are ungrouped, the procedure is the same as that explained in Chapter 6. You will be using the blue CFo and CFj keys in the top row of the keyboard. In addition, you will need to use the CHS key to enter outflows as negative numbers. Also, you will be entering the discount rate using the i key as usual. Finally, you will use the yellow f key and the NPV function to produce the solution.

To illustrate the process, assume you have been asked to make a $75,000 loan. The borrower agrees to the following repayment schedule:

End of year 1	$ 0
End of year 2	$15,000
End of year 3	$20,000
End of year 4	$25,000
End of year 5	$30,000

If you insist on a rate of return of at least 11 percent on your investment, should you enter into this loan? Press 75000, CHS, blue g, and CFo. The initial outlay (at the beginning of the first year) has now been entered as a negative amount. Press 0, blue g, and CFj to reflect the fact that in the first year following the initial outlay there is no net cash inflow or outflow. Press 15000, blue g, and CFj to enter the positive cash inflow at the end of year two. Enter the remaining three inflows by pressing 20000, blue g, CFj; 25000, blue g, CFj; and 30000, blue g, CFj. Now enter the minimum acceptable rate of return by pressing 11 and the i key. Finally, compute the NPV by pressing the yellow f key and NPV. The answer, −$13,930.02, appears on the display. Obviously this project should be rejected since, in light of the time value of money, it would cost you almost $14,000. This project would be unacceptable even if you were willing to settle for as little as a 5 percent rate of return. Press 5, i, yellow f, and NPV. Note that the net present value even at this rate is a negative $44.46.

Grouped Cash Flows

The HP-12C can solve NPV problems involving more than 20 cash flows beyond the initial one if there are grouped data, that is, if some of the consecutive cash flows are of the same sign and are of equal amounts. As was explained in Chapter 6, for such problems you should enter, along with the amount of each such cash flow, the total number of times it occurs in succession, including the first time. This is done by means of the blue Nj key.

To illustrate the process, assume that you are considering investing in an oil exploration limited partnership that you believe will entail the following cash flows:

Initial outlay	$50,000
Inflows at end of years 1-5	0
Inflows at end of years 6-9	$ 6,000
Inflow at end of year 10	$60,000

Is this investment acceptable if you insist on a rate of return of at least 12 percent per year?

After clearing the machine, begin by entering the amount of the initial outflow: 50000, CHS, blue g, and CFo. Now enter the first group of inflows by pressing 0, blue g, and CFj. Since this amount will occur a total of five times (including the first), press 5, blue g, and Nj. Now enter the next group of inflows: 6000, blue g, CFj, and the number of times it will occur: 4, blue g, Nj. Then enter the last inflow, 60000, blue g, CFj. Finally, enter the required interest rate by pressing 12 and i. Compute the answer by pressing yellow f and NPV and the answer, −$20,340.76, appears on the screen. Another great investment to be avoided!

COMPUTING INTERNAL RATE OF RETURN

Recall the definition of the second technique for discounted cash flow analysis. The internal rate of return generated by an investment is the interest rate that equates the present value of the cash inflows and outflows, producing a net present value of zero. If the IRR exceeds the investor's minimum desired rate of return, the investment is an attractive one. If it equals the minimum desired rate, the investor should be neutral toward the project. If the IRR is below the minimum desired rate, the investment is unattractive.

The mathematics of computing the IRR of an investment are extremely complex. The process is essentially one of trial and error. To solve the problem manually, you must begin with an estimate of what the IRR might be.[2] Some authors suggest that a rate such as 10 percent or 15 percent is usually a reasonable starting point. The cash inflows and outflows are then discounted to their present values using that rate and compared. If the present value of the inflows exceeds the present value of the outflows (that is, if there is a positive NPV at that rate), the rate being used is below the actual IRR, so you must select a higher rate and repeat the calculations. (Remember that present values move in a direction opposite that of interest rates. Here you are looking for a smaller net present value, namely, zero, so you must increase the interest rate being used.) On the other hand, if with a given interest rate the discounted cash outflows exceed the discounted cash inflows (that is, if there is a negative NPV), you must select a lower interest rate and repeat the calculations. Continue this trial and error process, using higher and lower interest rates to discount the cash flows, until the resulting

NPV is equal to or very close to zero. The rate producing this result is the IRR, which is an average rate of return over the period under consideration, weighted to reflect the amount and timing of the various cash flows.

Using a Time Value Table

Time value tables can be used to solve only very simple IRR problems. To illustrate, assume that an investment today of $10,000 will produce cash inflows of $2,739.80 at the end of each of the next 5 years. What is the internal rate of return on this investment?

Begin with a guess that it is 10 percent. At that rate and using table A.4 in Appendix A you will find that the present value of the annuity in this problem is ($2,739.80 x 3.7908 =) $10,386.03. The net present value is positive (namely, $386.03), so you need to raise the discount rate and redo the calculation. At a rate of 12.5 percent the PVA is ($2,739.80 x 3.5606 =) $9,755.33, so the NPV is now negative. Try 11 percent, and you will find that the NPV is ($2,739.80 x 3.6959 − $10,000 =) $126.03. You are getting closer, so try a rate of 11.5 percent. Here the present value of the inflows is ($2,739.80 x 3.6499 =) $10,000.00. Bingo! The internal rate of return is 11.5 percent.

Obviously the process of computing the internal rate of return is extremely tedious if done in this manner. Imagine, for example, if the project involved a series of uneven cash outflows, a lengthy series of uneven cash inflows, and an occasional year of zero inflows or outflows. By the time you finished doing and redoing and re-redoing all the computations, the investment opportunity would have passed you by.

Also, of course, it is impossible to calculate very precise IRR answers using tables A.2 and A.4. They show an array of interest rates only in intervals of a half percentage point. A process of interpolation would be needed to come closer to the precise IRR if it didn't happen to fall neatly on one of the tabular rates.

Using the BA-II

The BA-II financial calculator can be of a little help in calculating the IRR of an investment. As a practical matter, however, it is useable only for the most straightforward type of problem, that in which a single initial cash outflow is followed by an unbroken series of cash inflows of a single amount.

For example, assume that the purchase by a small business of a $12,000 piece of equipment will generate additional profits of $3,500 per year for 7 years, after which it will have no salvage value. This problem is identical to a debt service problem described in Chapter 5. There the task was, given the loan amount, the amount of the periodic payment, and the number of periods, to compute the interest rate. In the present case the task is, given the initial outlay, the amount of the periodic inflows, and the number of periods, to compute the internal rate of return. To solve the problem, set the calculator to display four decimal places. Then press the following keys: 12000, PV, 3500, PMT, 7, N, 2nd, and %i. After a few seconds the IRR, 21.8560 percent, will appear on the display.

For any type of IRR problem other than this basic one, the BA-II is not equipped to provide a solution readily. The only practical method of computing the internal rate of return for most investments, then, is to use a more sophisticated calculator such as the HP-12C or, for problems which exceed the capacity of the HP-12C, a computer.

Using the HP-12C

The procedure for solving IRR problems on the HP-12C is very similar to that for NPV problems. The use of the blue CFo, CFj, and Nj keys to enter the outflows (via the CHS key) and inflows is exactly as was explained earlier in this chapter. The only differences in the procedure are these:

1. When solving for IRR you do not need to enter a discount rate, since this is what you are trying to find. Therefore, skip the next to last step of the NPV sequence.

2. Instead of pressing yellow f and the NPV function after all the data have been entered, press yellow f and the IRR function, which is located on the FV key.

For example, to solve an earlier illustrative problem (a single outflow of $10,000 followed by five inflows of $2,739.80 each), set the calculator to display four decimal places. Then press the following keys: 10000, CHS, blue g, CFo, 2739.80, blue g, CFj, 5, blue g, Nj, yellow f, and IRR. (Normally it will be necessary for you to wait for several seconds for the answer to appear because of the complex mathematical characteristics of the IRR calculation.) Eventually the answer, 11.4997 percent, will be displayed on the screen. (Note the added precision of the HP-12C versus table A.4.) In fact if you set the calculator to display eight decimal places, its maximum capacity in this case, you would see that the IRR is 11.49974092 percent.)

Or to take a more involved example, assume that an investment you are considering involves a $60,000 initial outlay and then the following series of cash flows:

End of Year	Cash Flow	End of Year	Cash Flow
1	$2,000 inflow	6	$10,000 outflow
2	$9,000 inflow	7	$11,000 inflow
3	$9,000 inflow	8	0
4	$9,000 inflow	9	$12,000 inflow
5	$9,000 inflow	10	$30,000 inflow

The keystrokes would be as follows:

Initial outlay	60000, CHS, blue g, CFo,
year 1	2000, blue g, CFj,
years 2-5	9000, blue g, CFj, 4, blue g, Nj,
year 6	10000, CHS, blue g, CFj,
year 7	11000, blue g, CFj,
year 8	0, blue g, CFj,
year 9	12000, blue g, CFj,
year 10	30000, blue g, CFj,

Then press the yellow f key and IRR. After the machine runs for several seconds the answer, 4.6664 percent, will be displayed.

7.12

PROBLEMS IN DECISION MAKING BASED ON IRR

The internal rate of return provided by potential investments must be used with caution as a basis for decision making. This is especially true when the IRR is used as a means of ranking competing investment opportunities as to their relative attractiveness.

One situation in which an evaluation based solely on comparative IRRs may lead to an incorrect decision is the case of mutually exclusive investment projects that are of substantially different magnitudes.

Assume, for example, that you can invest in either of two pieces of equipment for your business, but that investment in one would eliminate the possibility of investing in the other for some technical reason. Assume also that you have or can borrow enough money so that you are free to invest in either type of equipment. The total cash flows from the two projects, A and B, are as shown below, and neither piece of equipment will have any salvage value.

Beginning of Year	Cash Flow (A)	Cash Flow (B)
1	$5,000 outflow	$50,000 outflow
2	$3,000 inflow	$25,000 inflow
3	$4,000 inflow	$35,000 inflow
4	$5,000 inflow	$45,000 inflow

The IRR from project A is 54.0603 percent, while that from project B is only 42.9811 percent. Does this mean that project A is preferable? Not necessarily. For example, if the money to meet the initial outflow is to be borrowed at a 10 percent rate of interest, it may be preferable to invest in project B. On the basis of a 10 percent discount rate, the NPV of project B is $35,462.06, whereas that of project A is only $4,789.63. In other words, project B would increase your wealth (in a time value sense) by more than seven times the increase that project A would provide. A more modest rate of return on a large project may be preferable to a higher rate of return on a small project. (Note, however, that this illustration deals with *mutually exclusive* projects. In other types of cases the wise decision might be to invest in both projects.)

A second type of situation in which a decision based solely on IRR may be incorrect is that in which mutually exclusive potential investment projects entail substantially different cash flow patterns. Assume that two competing investment opportunities, C and D, are expected to produce the total cash flows shown below. Assume also that the two projects are mutually exclusive because you are able to borrow only $30,000, the amount of the initial cash outlay for each. The interest rate the lender will charge and, therefore, the discount rate you have decided to use in evaluating the two projects is 12 percent per year.

Beginning of Year	Cash Flow (C)	Cash Flow (D)
1	$30,000 outflow	$30,000 outflow
2-5	$11,000 inflow	$5,000 inflow
6-20	0	$5,000 inflow

The IRR from project C is 17.2968 percent, while that from project D is only 15.6071 percent. The NPV of project D, however, is $6,828.88 at a discount rate of 12 percent, whereas it is only

$3,410.84 for project C. Once again, the project with the lower IRR provides a greater addition to your wealth (in a time value sense).

If all of that isn't sufficiently confusing, try a different discount rate, such as 19 percent, for the calculation of the NPV of the two projects. Under that assumption, project C has both the better IRR and the better (actually, the less bad) NPV.

There is another difficulty in relying solely on IRRs when deciding between investment opportunities with substantially different durations. The IRR method includes no explicit assumption about the rate of return at which funds released from a short duration project will be able to be reinvested. In the preceding example, project D will generate an annual IRR of over 15 percent for 19 years. Project C provides an annual IRR of a bit over 17 percent, but for only 4 years. Assume that the rates of return available on investments of comparable risk fall substantially during the next few years. This means that the heavy early cash inflows from project C will have to be reinvested at rates so unattractive that the combined IRR from project C and its successor(s) over the full 19 years will be less than its 4-year IRR, and perhaps even less than the 19-year IRR of project D.

Still another limitation of the IRR method for comparing investment projects is similar to the last one but involves a question of the cost of financing cash outflows that may be associated with one or both of the projects. Consider the following set of cash flows from investment projects E and F.

Beginning of Year	Cash Flow (E)	Cash Flow (F)
1	$10,000 outflow	$10,000 outflow
2	$ 1,000 inflow	0
3	$ 5,000 outflow	0
4	$ 5,000 inflow	0
5	$ 5,000 inflow	0
6	$ 5,000 inflow	$ 3,000 inflow
7	$ 5,000 inflow	$13,000 inflow

On the surface, project E appears to be clearly preferable. Its IRR appears to be (more on that below) 9.7283 percent versus 8.4315 percent for project F. And if a reasonable discount rate is used, such as 8 percent, for calculating NPV, project E wins again, $837.31 versus $233.95.

But notice that project E requires a $5,000 cash outflow at the beginning of year three. Presumably that amount will have to be borrowed at some rate of interest or taken out of some other investment where it is earning some rate of return. In either case there is a cost to the investor, either a direct cost or an opportunity cost, arising from the need to cover the cash outflow. If interest rates should rise substantially during the first 2 years of the project, that cost alone might be sufficient to drive the actual IRR of project E below that of project F.

A final problem to be discussed here concerning the IRR method is that it is possible for a project to have more than one IRR, each of which is mathematically correct. It is also possible that an investment may have no IRR within the realm of real numbers. A mathematical explanation of how these results can be produced is beyond the scope of this book. They can arise, however, whenever the stream of outflows and inflows involves more than one change of sign between negative and positive (for example, one or more outflows followed by one or more inflows followed by one or more outflows, as was the case in connection with project E above).

How can you tell whether an investment may have more than one internal rate of return? Look over the pattern of net cash outflows and inflows. Often there will be only one change of sign in these net flows over the lifetime of the investment. The sequence might begin with one or a few periods of net cash outflows (minus signs) which are followed by a series of net cash inflows (plus signs), perhaps with an occasional net inflow of zero (still a plus sign), until the project is concluded. Where there is only one sign change, there is only one internal rate of return. If there is more than one sign change, however, there *may* be more than one IRR, or there may be no IRR at all. All of the answers will be mathematically correct--and none of them will be of much help as a basis for making an intelligent decision.[3]

If you are using the HP-12C to compute the IRR of an investment, the calculator will usually let you know if it is having trouble computing the one and only correct internal rate of return. Any of the following results will appear on the display if a problem involves more than one sign change.

1. A positive answer, such as the 9.7283 percent IRR from project E above. This is the only *positive* IRR. In rare cases it is possible that a negative IRR may exist, although this is unlikely.

2. A negative answer. For example, compute IRR when the following is the sequence of cash flows: −$1,000; +$300; +$300; −$200; +$500. The answer will be shown on the display as a negative number, probably −3.9763 percent. In this case you cannot be sure of the answer. There *may* be multiple IRRs.

3. Error 3. For example, compute IRR when the following is the sequence of cash flows: −$1,000; +$125; −$250; +$500, −$300; −$500; +$500. The Error 3 message means that there may be multiple IRRs. The calculator is unable to sort out the answer unless you give the calculator an estimate of what the IRR is. Enter a guess, such as 15 percent, by pressing 15 and i. Then press RCL in the bottom row of the keyboard, blue g, and the R/S key in the left hand column of the keyboard. The calculator will resume the search (eventually deciding on an IRR of −28.7501 percent in this case).

What do you do about all these problems in using IRR as a basis for deciding about an investment? One simple solution is to punt. Perhaps you should forget about trying to use IRR as a method of evaluating the particular investment. Rather, use the NPV method. Another approach is to use one of several *modified* IRR methods that have been developed. Many textbooks on investments and managerial finance are available which contain explanations of these modified IRR methods, only one of which will be discussed in this book.

COMPUTING MODIFIED INTERNAL RATE OF RETURN[4]

The modified internal rate of return (MIRR) method described below attempts to deal with several of the limitations of the regular IRR technique. It does so by the following:

1. introducing a specific assumption as to the rate of return that presumably will be earned on reinvested funds;

2. introducing a specific assumption as to the interest cost that will be incurred in order to cover cash outflows; and

3. eliminating the possibility of multiple internal rates of return by grouping the cash inflows and outflows so that there is only one sign change.

The procedure involves first selecting a realistic rate of return at which the investor estimates that he or she would reinvest future cash inflows from the project as they are received. All the projected inflows are then grouped together and carried to their future value at that rate as of the end of the investment holding period (or as of the end of the holding period of a competing, longer-duration investment with which this one is being compared).

Next, the investor selects a rate of return which he or she estimates will be earned on supplemental funds placed on deposit at the inception of the investment project to meet future cash outflows as they arise. In most cases this should be a "safe" rate, a conservative rate to reflect the fact that usually the investor will want to be certain that he or she will be able to cover the net cash outflows as they occur. If so, the figure used might be the rate available on a passbook savings account. All the outflows are then grouped together and carried to their present value at the stipulated rate as of the beginning of the investment holding period.

The final step is to compute the interest rate which equates the present value of all the outflows, discounted at the investor-stipulated safe rate, to the future value of all the inflows, compounded at the investor-stipulated reinvestment rate. That rate, the MIRR, produces an adjusted NPV of zero.

In effect the MIRR method converts the terms of the investment being considered to a hypothetical one which includes one or more supplementary side funds of invested or reinvested money. The MIRR is, then, the IRR of the hypothetical combined fund.

Calculating MIRR on the HP-12C

Assume an investment in real estate can be made for an initial outlay of $100,000. The anticipated rental income from the property, net of expenses, for the next 10 years is $20,000 per year except at the end of year two, at which time needed repairs will produce a net cash outflow of $25,000 for the year. It is anticipated that the property can be sold at the end of the 10th year for $130,000. What is the IRR? What is the MIRR if a safe rate of 6 percent and a reinvestment rate of 10 percent are assumed? Review the pattern of these cash flows as depicted in figure 7.4.

On the HP-12C the regular IRR can be found by the following sequence of keystrokes:

Initial outflow	100000, CHS, blue g, CFo,
Inflow, year 1	20000, blue g, CFj,
Outflow, year 2	25000, CHS, blue g, CFj,
Inflows, years 3-9	20000, blue g, CFj, 7, blue g, Nj,
Inflow, year 10	150000, (that is, $20,000 + $130,000), blue g, CFj,
Solution	yellow f, IRR

The answer, 14.7509 percent, will appear on the display. Of course you cannot be completely certain that this is the one and only IRR, since the sequence of net cash flows involved three sign changes.

Now compute the modified IRR. Assume that the second year outflow is to be met by adding to the initial investment an amount which, invested separately at a safe rate of 6 percent, will be sufficient to cover the outflow when it occurs. The PVSS of $25,000 discounted at 6 percent for 2 years is (25000, FV, 2, n, 6, i, PV) $22,249.91. Thus the modified present value of all the outflows is ($100,000 + $22,249.91 =) $122,249.91.

Next, reinvest and accumulate at the 10 percent reinvestment rate all the cash inflows until the end of the tenth year. Clear the machine. The inflow at the end of the first year is a single sum the future value of which will be (20000, CHS, PV, 9, n, 10, i, FV) $47,158.95 at the end of year 10. Clear the machine. The inflows in years three through nine constitute an annuity the future value of which at the end of year nine will be (20000, CHS, PMT, 10, i, 7, n, blue g, END, FV) $189,743.42. Clear the machine. One year later, at the end of year 10, this single sum will have grown to (189743.42, CHS, PV, 10, i, 1, n, FV) $208,717.76.

FIGURE 7.4

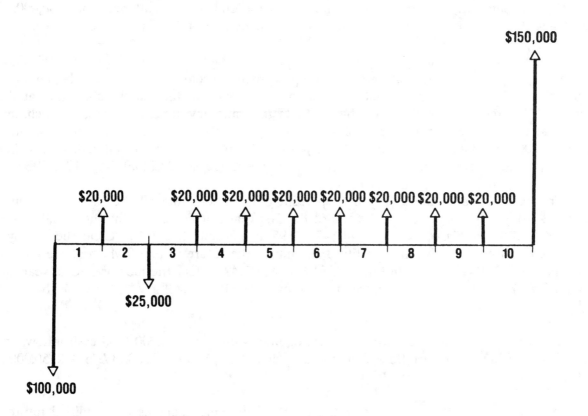

Figure 7.4. *Time Line Depiction of a Real Estate Investment.* This time line depicts a common sequence of cash outflows in a real estate investment situation--a large initial outlay of cash, followed by cash inflows from rental income, perhaps interrupted occasionally by a net cash outflow, and a large cash inflow when the property is sold.

Add the future value of these two annuities together with the $150,000 final cash inflow, and the modified future value of all the inflows from the project is ($47,158.95 + $208,717.76 + $150,000.00 =) $405,876.71.

Now comes the final step, determining the interest rate which equates the modified future value of the investment's aggregate inflows with the modified present value of the investment's aggregate outflows. This is the type of problem that was explained in Chapter 2: given PVSS, FVSS, and n, solve for i. Therefore clear the machine and set it to display four decimal places. Then press the following keys: 122249.91, CHS, PV, 405876.71, FV, 10, n, and i. The answer, the MIRR, is displayed as 12.7495 percent. Note that the MIRR is lower than the 14.7509 percent IRR because of the combination of the conservative 10 percent reinvestment rate assumed in the MIRR calculation and the 6 percent discounting of the negative cash flow in the second year.[5]

Calculating MIRR on the BA-II

The BA-II can also be used in fairly simple problems to calculate a project's modified internal rate of return. Assume an investment in real estate can be made for an initial outlay of $100,000. The anticipated rental income from the property, net of expenses, for the next 10 years is $20,000 per year except in year two, at which time needed repairs will produce a net cash outflow of $25,000 for the year. It is anticipated that the property can be sold at the end of the tenth year for $130,000. What is the MIRR if a safe rate of 6 percent and a reinvestment rate of 10 percent are assumed?

Review the pattern of these cash flows as depicted in figure 7.4. To begin the calculation of MIRR, first group all the cash outflows and compute their present value as of the beginning of the investment's holding period. Note that there is one outflow other than at the start, that at the end of year two. Assume that it is to be met by adding to the initial investment an amount which, invested separately at a safe rate of 6 percent, will be sufficient to cover that outflow when it occurs. The PVSS of $25,000 discounted at 6 percent for 2 years is (25000, FV, 2, N, 6, %i, 2nd, PV) $22,249.91. Thus the modified present value of all the outflows is ($100,000 + $22,249.91 =) $122,249.91.

Next, reinvest and accumulate at the 10 percent reinvestment rate all the cash inflows until the end of the tenth year. The inflow at the end of the first year is a single sum the future value of which will be (20000, PV, 10, %i, 9, N, 2nd, FV) $47,158.95 at the end of year 10. Clear the display. The inflows in years three through nine constitute an annuity the future value of which at the end of year nine will be (20000, PMT, 7, N, 10, %i, 2nd, FV) $189,743.42. Clear the memory. One year later, at the end of year 10, this single sum will have grown to (189743.42, PV, 10, %i, 1, N, 2nd, FV) $208,717.76.

Add the future value of these two annuities together with the $150,000 final cash inflow, and the modified future value of all the inflows from the project is ($47,158.95 + $208,717.76 + $150,000.00 =) $405,876.71.

Now comes the final step, determining the interest rate which equates the modified future value of the investment's aggregate inflows with the modified present value of the investment's aggregate outflows. This is the type of problem that was explained in Chapter 2: given PVSS, FVSS, and n, solve for i. Therefore clear the display and set the calculator to show four decimal places. Then press the following keys: 122249.91, PV, 405876.71, FV, 10, N, 2nd, and %i. The answer, the MIRR, is displayed as 12.7495 percent.

This investment, by the way, has a regular IRR of 14.7509 percent. The MIRR is lower because of the combination of the conservative 10 percent reinvestment rate assumed in the MIRR calculation and the 6 percent discounting of the negative cash flow in year two. (See also note 5 at the end of this chapter.)

NOTES

1. In this and in all investment opportunities being evaluated, care must be exercised to be sure that all relevant elements of the cash inflow and outflow streams are considered and discounted properly. Don't forget, for example, to include when appropriate such items as shipping and installation costs of a proposed new piece of equipment, maintenance costs, income taxes, salvage value, etc. In the illustrations in this chapter it is assumed that all such considerations have already been accounted for in the numbers being used.

2. As will be seen, this is not usually necessary when using the HP-12C calculator's IRR function.

3. For an interesting example of multiple IRRs, see Roger H. Allen, *Real Estate Investment and Taxation*. 2nd ed. (Cincinnati: South-Western Publishing Co., 1984), p. 205. There an illustration developed by Robert J. Doyle of the faculty of The American College is presented showing an investment that has several internal rates of return. The cash flows used in the illustration are ($1,000), $3,600, ($4,310), and $1,716. An investment with this set of cash flows has IRRs of 10 percent, 20 percent, and 30 percent. Each of those rates, when used to discount the cash flows, produces an NPV of zero.

4. This is the terminology used in the HP-12C manual. In the BA-II manual it is called the Modified Financial Management Rate of Return method.

5. Notice that in this and other illustrations where there is a gap between the reinvestment rate and the safe rate, the MIRR is a very conservative (understated) rate. A side fund invested at a low safe rate may be unnecessary because the inflows in early years, reinvested at a higher rate, may be more than sufficient to cover the later outflows.

PROBLEMS

1. You have just made a loan of $85,000 to a friend, who has agreed to the following repayment schedule:

End of year 1	$ 5,000
End of year 2	$ 10,000
End of year 3	0
End of year 4	0
End of year 5	$100,000

   (a) What is your internal rate of return?

   (b) What is the net present value of this investment if 10 percent is your minimum acceptable compound annual rate of return?

2. Tax reform legislation notwithstanding, you have located an exotic tax-sheltered investment opportunity. For an initial outlay of $50,000 and an additional $10,000 5 years from now, you will receive the following income stream:

End of years 1-4	$7,500
End of years 6-10	$8,000

   What is the internal rate of return on this investment?

3. You are debating whether to invest $100,000 in a piece of equipment that will produce the following cost savings for your business:

End of years 1-3	$30,000
End of year 4	($10,000)
End of years 5-7	$20,000

   (a) What is the internal rate of return?

   (b) What is the net present value if you discount the cash flows at the 8 percent compound annual interest rate you would have to pay in order to finance the purchase of the equipment?

   (c) What is the modified internal rate of return if a safe rate of 5 percent and a reinvestment rate of 12 percent are assumed?

SOLUTIONS

1. (a) Even for a fairly simple set of cash flows such as this one, the HP-12C is the most practical means of calculating the IRR. The keystrokes are as follows: 85000, CHS, blue g, CFo, 5000, blue g, CFj, 10000, blue g, CFj, 0, blue g, CFj, 2, blue g, Nj, 100000, blue g, CFj, yellow f, IRR. The answer is 6.9171%.

    (b) With the above data still in the machine, press 10, i, yellow f, NPV. The answer is −$10,097.95.

Alternatively, the NPV can be found by using present value factors from table A.2.

$5,000	x	.9091	=	$ 4,545.50	
$10,000	x	.8264	=	8,264.00	
$100,000	x	.6209	=	62,090.00	

Present value of inflows	$74,899.50
− Present value of outflows	85,000.00
Net present value	− $10,100.50

2. On the HP-12C press 50000, CHS, blue g, CFo, 7500, blue g, CFj, 4, blue g, Nj, 10000, CHS, blue g, CFj, 8000, blue g, CFj, 5, blue g, Nj, yellow f, IRR. The answer probably is 3.3231%. Because the income stream involves more than one sign change, however, there may also be a negative IRR, though this is unlikely.

3. (a) The internal rate of return may be found on the HP-12C by pressing 100000, CHS, blue g, CFo, 30000, blue g, CFj, 3, blue g, Nj, 10000, CHS, blue g, CFj, 20000, blue g, CFj, 3, blue g, Nj, yellow f, IRR. The answer is 10.6118% (but see solution 2 above).

    (b) With the above data still in the machine, press 8, i, yellow f, NPV. The answer is $7,847.48.

Alternatively, the NPV can be found by using PVSS and PVA factors from tables A.2 and A.4.

$30,000	x 2.5771		=	$ 77,313.00
$20,000	x 2.5771 x .7350		=	37,883.37
Present value of inflows				$115,196.37

$100,000	x 1.0000		=	$100,000.00
$10,000	x .7350		=	7,350.00
Present value of outflows				$107,350.00

Net present value	$7,846.37

(c) Based on a PVSS factor from table A.2, the modified present value of the outflows is $100,000 + ($10,000 x .8227), or $108,227. Based on FVSS and FVA factors from tables A.1 and A.3, the modified future value of the inflows is

$30,000	x 3.3744 x 1.5735	=	$159,288.55
$20,000	x 3.3744	=	67,488.00
Total			$226,776.55

With $108,227 as the PV, $226,776.55 as the FV, and 7 as the n, the i, the MIRR, is 11.1462%. If instead of using tables for part of the solution you use the HP-12C or BA-II throughout, the resulting MIRR is 11.1463%.

CHAPTER 8

INCREASING THE COMPOUNDING, DISCOUNTING, OR PAYMENT FREQUENCY

All the explanations and illustrations so far in this book have been based on the assumption that compounding and discounting to determine the time value of money occur once per year. In reality, however, compounding and discounting often occur more frequently than annually. For example, a certificate of deposit may be credited with compound interest on a monthly basis. A Super NOW account may earn daily compound interest. The present value of the income from a corporate bond typically is computed on the basis of semiannual discounting.

In addition, all of the explanations of problems involving periodic payments thus far in the book have been based on the assumption that the payments are made annually. Often however, such payments occur more than once per year. Installment loan payments, for example, often are made monthly. Bond interest payments usually are made every 6 months. Deposits into the savings accounts of many people are made weekly.

The present chapter examines the effect on the interest rate and, therefore, on the time value of money resulting from compounding or discounting more often than annually. It also contains an explanation of how to solve problems involving a series of level payments that occur more often than once per year, regardless of how often per year compounding or discounting takes place.

NOMINAL VERSUS EFFECTIVE INTEREST RATES

As you know, compounding results in the conversion of interest earnings into principal. For example, if $100 is deposited today and subsequently is credited with $7.00 of compound interest, the principal on which future interest will be credited rises to $107. The $7.00 of interest becomes converted into principal.

If compounding occurs annually, when does interest become converted into principal and begin to earn interest on itself? Obviously the conversion and, thus, the capacity for increased interest earnings occur after one year, again after 2 years, and so on. If, on the other hand, compounding occurs on, for example, a monthly basis, when does interest become converted to principal and thus begin to earn interest on itself? The conversions occur after one month has elapsed, again after 2 months, 3 months, etc.

Of course the greater the frequency with which compounding occurs, the smaller will be the dollar amount of interest earned and converted into principal on the occasion of each compounding. Naturally the amount of interest a given amount of principal can earn in a week, for example, is less than it can earn in a month at any given stated or nominal annual interest rate. Nevertheless, all other things being equal, the more frequently compounding occurs, the greater will be the *total* amount of interest credited to an account in a year. To illustrate, table 8.1 shows the amount of interest that will be credited during one year to a $5,000 deposit with a stated or nominal 9 percent annual interest rate if that 9 percent rate is applied with various frequencies during the year.

Technically, of course, compounding can occur even more frequently than daily--every hour, every minute, every second, or even more frequently than that. And as the frequency continues to increase, so does the total interest credited. The upper limit of the total interest credited to a sum of money for a particular stated or nominal annual interest rate occurs in the case of continuous compounding, wherein interest is compounded an infinite number of times per year, rather than at discrete time

TABLE 8.1
Total Interest Credited to a $5,000 Deposit during One Year at 9% Stated Annual Interest Rate and Various Compounding Frequencies

Compounding Frequency	Interest Earnings
Annually	$450.00
Semiannually	460.13
Quarterly	465.42
Monthly	469.03
Weekly	470.45
Daily*	470.81

*Based on 360 days per year.[1]

intervals. Continuous compounding is a theoretical concept useful principally in the study of advanced financial topics, but it also has some practical applications since financial institutions occasionally credit interest to customer accounts on a continuous basis.

From the figures in table 8.1 it should be obvious that a stated or nominal annual interest rate does not necessarily reflect the true or effective interest rate. You have seen that a 9 percent nominal annual rate produces any of six separate interest earnings in a year, depending on the frequency with which compounding occurs. Hence it is important to distinguish between the nominal or stated annual rate (9 percent in this illustration) and the true or effective annual rate.

When compounding occurs once per year, the nominal and effective annual rates are identical. In table 8.1 the $5,000 deposit earned $450, exactly 9 percent, when annual compounding was applied. In all other cases it earned more than $450, more than 9 percent, because compounding occurred more than once per year.

The effective annual interest rate is defined as the annual rate that would produce in one compounding the same amount of interest as does the nominal annual rate with its compounding frequency. For instance, the 9 percent nominal annual rate in table 8.1 when compounded quarterly produced $465.42 of interest. Thus the effective annual interest rate was ($465.42 ÷ $5,000 =) 9.3084 percent. Similarly, the 9 percent nominal annual rate compounded daily generated $470.81 of interest. Thus the effective annual rate was ($470.81 ÷ $5,000 =) 9.4332 percent.

CALCULATING THE EFFECTIVE ANNUAL RATE

The effective annual interest rate can be computed for any nominal rate and compounding frequency by the following formula:[2]

$$i_{eff} = \left[1 + \frac{i_{nom}}{f}\right]^f - 1$$

where i_{eff} is the effective annual rate

i_{nom} is the nominal annual rate

f is the compounding frequency per year

Thus, for example, a 9 percent nominal annual rate compounded monthly represents an effective annual rate of

$$\left[1 + \frac{.09}{12}\right]^{12} - 1$$

$$= 9.3807\%$$

As an alternative to using this formula, you can calculate the effective interest rate for any nominal annual rate and compounding frequency by using the HP-12C or BA-II calculator. To illustrate, assume that a 7 percent nominal rate is to be compounded weekly. Clear the HP-12C's registers and set the calculator to display four decimal places. Then press the following keys:

       blue g, END,
       7, ENTER, (to enter the nominal rate)
       52, n, ÷, i, (to enter the weekly frequency of compounding)
       100, CHS, ENTER, PV, FV, + (to produce the effective rate)

The answer, 7.2458 percent, appears on the display.

If you use the BA-II, clear the registers and set the calculator to display four decimal places. Then press the following keys:

       52, N, (to enter the weekly frequency of compounding)
       7, ÷, 52, =, %i, (to adjust the nominal annual rate to a weekly rate)
       1, PV, 2nd, FV, 1, N, 2nd, %i (to produce the effective rate)

The answer, 7.2458 percent, appears on the display.

For those who do not wish to use either a formula or a financial calculator to determine the effective interest rate, Appendix D at the end of this book will be of some help. It contains a table showing the effective annual interest rate that corresponds to a number of nominal annual rates and commonly-used compounding frequencies. The table includes the effective rate for the unusual case of continuous compounding.

To illustrate further the difference between the nominal and effective annual rates of interest, the following list shows the effective rate for a nominal rate of 7 percent with various compounding frequencies.

7% annually	=	7.0000%	effective rate
7% semiannually	=	7.1225%	effective rate
7% quarterly	=	7.1859%	effective rate
7% monthly	=	7.2290%	effective rate
7% weekly	=	7.2458%	effective rate
7% daily (360)	=	7.2501%	effective rate

Again it is clear that, for a particular nominal annual interest rate, the true or effective rate rises as the frequency of compounding per year increases. Note, however, that the increase in the effective rate becomes smaller and smaller with each increase in compounding frequency. In the above list, for example, the change from annual to semiannual compounding increased the effective rate by (7.1225 − 7.0000 =) .1225 percentage points. The change from semiannual to quarterly compounding changed the effective rate by only (7.1859 − 7.1225 =) .0634 percentage points; and the change from quarterly to monthly compounding increased it by only (7.2290 − 7.1859 =) .0431 percentage points.

Another point worth noting concerning nominal versus effective annual interest rates is that sometimes a low nominal rate with a high compounding frequency will produce a higher effective rate than a higher nominal rate with a lower compounding frequency. For example, assume that you plan to deposit $10,000 in an interest-bearing account for one year. Bank A pays interest of 8 percent compounded semiannually. Bank B pays 7.9 percent compounded daily (360 days per year). Where should you put your money? If you were to use the formula described earlier or a financial calculator, you would find that the effective rate in Bank A is 8.1600 percent. Bank B, on the other hand, pays an effective rate of 8.2195 percent. That is an extra $5.95 that will be credited to your $10,000 deposit if you go to Bank B.

IMPACT OF COMPOUNDING FREQUENCY ON FUTURE VALUES

Because the effective interest rate rises as the frequency of compounding of a particular nominal annual interest rate increases, so does the future value of a single sum. The same is true of other future values described in this book. For example, the future value of an annual annuity or of a series of annual uneven cash flows rises as compounding frequency increases. Conversely, in sinking fund problems as described in Chapter 4 the size of the annual payment needed to reach a targeted future amount diminishes as the frequency of compounding and the effective interest rate increase. Finally, the number of years or of annual payments needed to reach a particular future value decreases as the frequency of compounding and the effective interest rate increase.

IMPACT OF DISCOUNTING FREQUENCY ON PRESENT VALUES

You probably have already guessed that increasing the frequency of discounting has the opposite effect on present values from the effect that increasing the frequency of compounding has on future values. This again follows from the preceding discussion of nominal versus effective interest rates.

To illustrate, calculate the present value of $100 due in one year at 7 percent. Discounted annually, you know that the effective rate is 7 percent. The present value of $100 for one year at 7 percent is $93.46. Discounted quarterly, however, the effective rate is 7.1859 percent. The present value of $100 for one year at 7.1859 percent is $93.30. And discounted monthly the effective rate is 7.2290 percent, which produces a present value of $93.26. Generalizing from these results, then, you can conclude that, all other things being equal, an increase in the frequency with which discounting occurs increases the effective interest rate and, therefore, reduces the present value of a single sum. The same is true of the present value of an annual annuity or of a series of annual uneven cash flows. Conversely, in debt service problems as described in Chapter 5, an increase in the frequency of charging interest per year, all other things being equal, increases the amount of the loan payments per year. Finally, the number of years it will take to pay off a loan or to liquidate a principal sum increases as the frequency of charging or crediting interest per year increases, all other things being equal.

CALCULATING FUTURE AND PRESENT VALUES

When you encounter a time value of money problem in which the interest rate is compounded or discounted more than once per year there are two basic ways of solving it: using the effective rate or adjusting the nominal rate and number of periods.

Using the Effective Rate

The first basic approach is to begin solving the problem by computing the effective interest rate as explained earlier in this chapter. Then use the effective rate in the same way as you have learned to use the nominal annual interest rate throughout this book.

For example, to what amount will $500 grow in 3 years at 6 percent compounded quarterly? The effective rate is 6.13636 percent. Therefore you can use this rate in place of 6 percent in the FVSS formula. Specifically,

$$FVSS = \$500 \ (1.0613636)^3$$

$$= \$500 \times 1.19562$$

$$= \$597.81$$

Or what is the present value of a 5-year annuity of $2,000 if it is discounted at 8 percent weekly? The effective rate is 8.32205 percent. Therefore you can use this rate in place of 8 percent in the PVA formula. Specifically,

$$PVA = \left[\frac{1 - \left[\frac{1}{(1.0832205)^5} \right]}{.0832205} \right] \times \$2,000$$

$$= \left[\frac{1 - \left[\frac{1}{1.49137} \right]}{.0832205} \right] \times \$2,000$$

$$= \left[\frac{1 - .67053}{.0832205} \right] \times \$2,000$$

$$= 3.9590 \times \$2,000$$

$$= \$7,918$$

Instead of using a formula, you can solve these problems by means of your financial calculator. Again, however, you should first calculate the effective rate. Then follow the normal series of keystrokes for the particular type of problem, but insert the effective rate, rather than the nominal rate, into the calculator as the interest rate.

Using a present value or future value table usually is infeasible if you follow this first method. Most such tables, including those in Appendix A of this book, fail to provide factors for the fine gradations of effective interest rates that would be needed. For example, there is no set of FVSS factors in table A.1 for an interest rate of 6.13636 percent. Similarly, there is no set of PVA factors in table A.4 for an interest rate of 8.32205 percent.

Adjusting the Nominal Rate and Number of Periods

The second basic way of solving these kinds of problems involves using the nominal annual rate, rather than the effective rate. In this case, however, two adjustments must be made. First, the nominal annual interest rate in the problem must be *divided* by the number of compounding or discounting periods per year. This reflects the fact that only a fraction of the annual rate will be applied each time compounding or discounting occurs during the year. Second, the number of years in the problem must be *multiplied* by the number of compounding or discounting periods per year. This reflects the total number of times during the period covered by the problem that compounding or discounting of the fractional annual rate will occur. Note, then, that if this approach is used the number which is divided into i and the number which is multiplied by n are always the same (4 for quarterly compounding or discounting, 12 for monthly, 360 for daily, etc.)

To illustrate this approach to solving time value problems, compute the FVSS of $100 at 8 percent compounded quarterly for 20 years. Instead of the usual formula

$$FVSS = \$100 \ (1.08)^{20} = \$466.10$$

the formula becomes

$$FVSS = \$100 \ (1.02)^{80} = \$487.54$$

That is, the 8 percent annual rate was divided by 4 and the 20-year period was multiplied by 4.

Or if you wish to calculate by means of the formula the present value of $3,000 due 6 years hence with a discount rate of 12 percent applied monthly, the usual formula

$$PVSS = \$3,000 \left[\frac{1}{(1.12)^6} \right] = \$1,519.89$$

is replaced by

$$PVSS = \$3,000 \left[\frac{1}{(1.01)^{72}} \right] = \$1,465.49$$

That is, the 12 percent annual rate was divided by 12 and the 6-year period was multiplied by 12.

If you prefer to use tables rather than formulas to calculate present and future values, the same two adjustments must be made. For example, if the nominal annual interest rate in a problem is 6 percent, the number of years is 1, and compounding occurs quarterly, use the tabular factor not for 6 percent and one period but that for (6% ÷ 4 =) 1.5 percent and (1 x 4 =) 4 periods. Or if a problem involves a nominal rate of 9 percent, discounting occurs semiannually, and the number of years is 8, use the tabular factor not for 9 percent and 8 periods but that for (9% ÷ 2 =) 4.5 percent and (8 x 2 =) 16 periods.

One difficulty you may encounter in attempting to use tables in this way is that the adjusted nominal rate may not be presented there. For example, an 11 percent rate that is compounded monthly would require a set of factors for an adjusted nominal rate of 9.1667 percent. A 12 percent nominal rate that is compounded weekly would require a set of factors for an adjusted nominal rate of .2308 percent. There is no easy way to overcome this difficulty.

A second difficulty you may encounter in using the tables is that, when n is multiplied by the number of compounding or discounting periods in a year, the resulting number of periods may be greater than those shown in the table. For example, assume you wish to calculate the future value at the end of 5 years at 18 percent of a $2,000 single sum on the basis of monthly compounding. The factor needed from table A.1 is that for (18% ÷ 12 =) 1.5 percent and (5 x 12 =) 60 periods. The table, however, shows factors for only as high as 50 periods. This difficulty can be overcome simply by multiplying together the factors for any two years in the 1.5 percent column for which the combined number of periods is equal to the desired number, 60. For example, multiply the factor for 50 years by that for 10 years to produce a 60-year FVSS factor at 1.5 percent of (2.1052 x 1.1605 =) 2.4431. This, multiplied by $2,000, produces the FVSS, $4,886.17. The same technique may be used in conjunction with table A.2 to compute the factor for any number of periods needed to solve an FVSS problem. *It cannot be used in this way, however, to solve annuity problems through tables A.2 or A.4.*

Assume that instead of formulas or tables you wish to use a financial calculator. The only new procedure when using the BA-II for problems involving compounding more often than annually is to make the two adjustments referred to above: divide the nominal annual i by the compounding frequency and multiply the number of years by the compounding frequency. These adjustments may by made mentally before data are entered or they may be made on the calculator itself as part of the data entry process. The latter approach will be illustrated here because the numbers to be used will be a bit too complex to deal with mentally.

Assume you wish to know the amount to which $15,000 will grow in 4 years at an 8 percent nominal annual interest rate if compounding occurs on a weekly basis. The solution process entails entering the initial sum as a present value, entering 4 years of weekly compounding as the number of periods, and entering 1/52 of 8 percent as the weekly interest rate. To solve the problem on the BA-II press the following keys:

> 15000, PV, (to enter the initial deposit)
> 4, x, 52, =, N, (to enter the number of compounding periods)
> 8, ÷, 52, =, %i, (to enter the weekly interest rate)
> 2nd, FV (to produce the solution)

The answer, $20,651.84, appears on the display screen.

The sequence of keystrokes for solving this problem on the HP-12C is somewhat similar.

> 15000, CHS, PV, (to enter the initial deposit)
> 4, ENTER, 52, x, n, (to enter the number of compounding periods)
> 8, ENTER, 52, ÷, i, (to enter the weekly interest rate)
> FV (to produce the solution)

The answer, $20,651.84, is displayed.

The HP-12C has one additional feature which is a useful shortcut when solving problems involving monthly compounding (or discounting). Note that the n key also has a blue 12x function and the i key has a blue 12÷ function. These serve to automatically adjust n and i to a monthly basis.

To illustrate, assume you wish to calculate the payment amount at the end of each month on a $9,000, 4-year automobile loan carrying a nominal annual interest rate of 8.8 percent compounded monthly. Press the following keys:

> blue g, END, (to set the payment mode to the end of the month)
> 9000, CHS, PV, (to enter the loan amount)
> 8.8, blue g, i, (to enter the monthly interest rate)
> 4, blue g, n, (to enter the number of payments)
> PMT (to produce the solution)

The answer, $223.11, appears on the display.

INTERPRETING THE RESULTS OF THE CALCULATIONS

When the solution to a time value of money problem is a value for i, n, or PMT, remember that these are *periodic* values. Therefore, if the compounding or discounting frequency is other than annual, for example, quarterly, these solutions also are other-than-annual values, namely, quarterly in this case. To convert the solution to an annual basis, therefore, it must be multiplied by, in the case of quarterly results, 4.

For example, assume you wish to compute the annual interest rate on a $1,000 loan that calls for 12 monthly payments of $99, beginning one month from the date of the loan. When you enter the data into your calculator, you will initially find as the solution a rate of 2.7553 percent. This, however, is a monthly rate. Multiply it by 12 to find the annual rate, 33.0631 percent. A similar procedure is used to convert a computed value of n or PMT to an annual basis.

ANNUITY PAYMENTS OCCURRING OTHER THAN ANNUALLY

Thus far in this chapter we have examined problems in which compounding or discounting occurs more frequently than once per year. A related but separate topic is the question of annuity payments that occur more frequently than once per year. (Uneven cash flows that occur other than annually are not dealt with in this book.)

Simple Annuities and Simple Annuities Due

A simple annuity or annuity due is one in which the frequency of payments and the frequency of compounding or discounting are identical. For example, a series of six quarterly deposits that are credited with interest quarterly and that begin 3 months from now is a simple annuity. Likewise, a series of 15 monthly payments that are discounted on a monthly basis and that begin immediately is a simple annuity due. All of the topics discussed in Chapters 4 and 5 involved simple annuities or simple annuities due because both the payment frequency and the compounding or discounting frequency were identical, once per year.

The calculation of the present or future value of a simple annuity or a simple annuity due when payments are more frequent than annual involves the same tools as you have already learned. The same formulas you used for computing FVA, FVAD, PVA, and PVAD can be used; the same FVA and PVA tables can be used; the same keystrokes can be used on the HP-12C or the BA-II—*except for two adjustments*. First, the figure to be used as the n should always be the total number of *payments* in the problem, not the number of years. Second, the figure to be used as the i should always be the *periodic* interest rate, not the annual rate. For example, in a problem that involves 3 years of quarterly payments and a 16 percent interest rate compounded quarterly, n is 12 and i is 4 percent. Or in one that involves 5 years of monthly payments and a 6 percent interest rate compounded monthly, n is 60 and i is .5 percent.

You can also calculate the n, i, or PMT in a simple annuity or annuity due involving other-than-annual payments. Use the same tools as you would have used if the payments had been annual. Again, however, the item you input or compute as n will always be the total number of payments, not the total number of years. The item you input or compute as i will always be the periodic interest rate, not the annual rate. And the item you input or compute as PMT will always be the single periodic payment, not the sum of the payments per year.

Complex Annuities and Complex Annuities Due

A complex annuity or annuity due is one in which the frequency of payments and the frequency of compounding or discounting are different. For example, a series of 14 monthly deposits that are credited with interest daily and that begin immediately is a complex annuity due. Likewise, a series of 10 semiannual lease payments that are discounted on an annual basis and that begin 6 months from now is a complex annuity.

The mathematics of solving problems involving complex annuities are fairly complex and generally beyond the scope of this book. Here we will deal with only two types of complex annuity problems, computing the FVA or FVAD and the PVA or PVAD. The tool described for finding the solution to each will be a formula, though a calculator will also be needed, especially to facilitate raising certain numbers to a power.

In order to solve problems involving complex annuities it is necessary to introduce one new variable that has not been used in any of the problems heretofore. That new variable, which we shall label as "c", is the number of times that compounding or discounting occurs *in each payment interval*. The value of c is found by dividing the frequency of compounding or discounting per year by the frequency of the payments per year. For example, if compounding occurs monthly and annuity payments are made quarterly, c = 3. Or if discounting occurs semiannually and annuity payments are made weekly, c = 1/26.

The formula for computing the future value of a complex annuity is presented below. In it, as in simple annuities, i is the periodic interest rate and n is the total number of annuity payments.

$$FVA = \left[\frac{(1 + i)^{n \times c} - 1}{(1 + i)^c - 1} \right] \text{(amount of one deposit)}$$

To illustrate, assume that $70 is deposited in a savings account every 6 months for 5 years. The first deposit is made 6 months from now. Interest is credited to the account at a 12 percent nominal annual rate, compounded monthly. How much will be in the account at the end of 5 years? Substituting in the formula, we have

$$FVA = \left[\frac{(1.01)^{10 \times 6} - 1}{(1.01)^6 - 1}\right](\$70)$$

$$= \left[\frac{.8167}{.0615}\right](\$70)$$

$$= (13.2797) \times \$70$$

$$= \$929.58$$

If in this illustration the first deposit were made immediately rather than 6 months from now, that is, if the problem called for finding FVAD, one further step would be necessary. The value of the FVA would have to be increased in a manner analogous to that used for annual annuities due. Specifically, the adjustment to be made is

$$FVAD = FVA \, (1 + i)^c$$

Again, remember to use the periodic interest rate for i in making this adjustment. In this illustration, then,

$$FVAD = \$929.58 \, (1.01)^6$$

$$= \$929.58 \times 1.0615$$

$$= \$986.75$$

That is, the account balance would be 6.15 percent higher because an extra 6 months of interest would be earned at a 12 percent nominal annual rate compounded monthly.

Next we will turn to calculating the present value of a complex annuity. The formula is presented below. As before, n is the total number of payments, i is the periodic interest rate, and c is the discounting frequency per payment interval.

$$PVA = \left[\frac{1 - \left[\frac{1}{(1 + i)^{n \times c}}\right]}{(1 + i)^c - 1}\right](\text{amount of one payment})$$

To illustrate, assume that during the first 3 1/2 years after you retire you want to have interest income of \$250 per month, beginning one month after your retirement date. Also assume that the principal sum to be liquidated in order to provide this income can be invested at a nominal annual rate of 6 percent, compounded quarterly. How large a principal sum will you need on the date you retire? What is the present value of this complex annuity? Substituting in the formula, we have

$$PVA = \left[\frac{1 - \left[\frac{1}{(1.015)^{42 \times 1/3}}\right]}{(1.015)^{1/3} - 1}\right](\$250)$$

$$= \left[\frac{(1 - .8118)}{(1.0050 - 1)}\right](\$250)$$

$$= 37.64 \times \$250$$

$$= \$9,410.00$$

If in this illustration the $250 of monthly income were to begin on your retirement date rather than one month later, that is, if the problem called for calculating the PVAD rather than the PVA, one further step would be necessary. The value of the PVA would have to be increased in a manner analogous to that used for annual annuities due. Specifically, the adjustment to be made is

$$PVAD = PVA \, (1 + i)^c$$

Again, remember to use the periodic interest rate in making this adjustment. In this illustration, then,

$$PVAD = \$9,410 \, (1.015)^{1/3}$$

$$= \$9,410 \, (1.0050)$$

$$= \$9,457.05$$

That is, the principal sum would have to be about .5 percent higher because one month of interest earnings would be lost on a 6 percent annual rate compounded quarterly.

NOTES

1. Financial institutions typically use a 360-day year as the basis for daily compounding calculations. This produces a slightly smaller annual interest, all other things being equal, than if they were to use a 365-day year.

2. The mathematics of calculating the effective rate manually when compounding is continuous are too complex to be dealt with in this book. The procedure for calculating it by using the HP-12C or BA-II calculators, however, is included in Appendices B and C.

PROBLEMS

1. Use the formula or your financial calculator to compute the effective annual interest rate when a nominal annual rate of 18 percent is compounded

   (a) semiannually
   (b) quarterly
   (c) monthly

   Check your answers by comparing them with table D.1 in the appendix.

2. Where should you put your money: in a certificate of deposit that will earn 9.75 percent compounded daily (360 days) or in one that will earn 10 percent compounded semiannually?

3. (a) Show which is the larger amount: the future value of a 10-year, $2,000 annual annuity growing at a nominal annual interest rate of 5 percent compounded weekly or one growing at a nominal annual interest rate of 5 percent compounded monthly.

   (b) Show which is the larger amount: the present value of a 6-year, $3,000 annual annuity discounted at 11 percent applied monthly or one discounted at 11 percent applied quarterly.

4. Assume that you plan to save for Junior's college education by depositing $200 per month for the next 12 years in a savings account, beginning immediately. The account is expected to earn a nominal annual rate of 6 percent, compounded monthly. How much will be in the account at the end of the twelfth year?

5. What is the present value of a stream of 10 quarterly payments of $500 each, beginning 3 months from now, if an annual discount rate of 16 percent is applied semiannually?

SOLUTIONS

1. (a) $\left[1 + \dfrac{.18}{2}\right]^2 -1 = 18.81000\%$

   (b) $\left[1 + \dfrac{.18}{4}\right]^4 -1 = 19.25186\%$

   (c) $\left[1 + \dfrac{.18}{12}\right]^{12} -1 = 19.56182\%$

2. Take the 10 percent rate. The 9.75 percent CD pays an effective rate of

$$\left[1 + \dfrac{.0975}{360}\right]^{360} -1 = 10.2397\%$$

whereas the 10 percent CD pays an effective rate of

$$\left[1 + \dfrac{.10}{2}\right]^2 -1 = 10.2500\%$$

3. (a) Weekly compounding will produce the larger FVA because the effective annual interest rate is 5.12458 percent, versus 5.11619 percent for monthly compounding. Substituting these effective rates in the FVA formula in Chapter 4, we have

$$\left[\dfrac{(1.0512458)^{10} -1}{.0512458}\right] (\$2,000) = \$25,302.55$$

versus

$$\left[\dfrac{(1.0511619)^{10} -1}{.0511619}\right] (\$2,000) = \$25,292.63$$

   (b) Discounting on a quarterly basis will produce the larger PVA. The effective rate for quarterly discounting is 11.46213 percent, versus 11.57188 percent for monthly discounting. Substituting these effective rates in the PVA formula in Chapter 5, we have

$$\left[\dfrac{1 -\left[\dfrac{1}{(1.1146213)^6}\right]}{.1146213}\right] (\$3,000) = \$12,524.43$$

versus

$$\left[\dfrac{1 -\left[\dfrac{1}{(1.1157188)^6}\right]}{.1157188}\right] (\$3,000) = \$12,485.24$$

4. If you use the FVAD formula from Chapter 4, the answer for this simple annuity is found as

$$= (1.005) \left[\frac{(1.005)^{144} - 1}{.005} \right] (\$200)$$

$$= (1.005) \left[\frac{1.0508}{.005} \right] \quad (\$200)$$

$$= 1.005 \times 210.16 \times \$200$$

$$= \$42,242.16$$

Table A.2 cannot be used to solve the problem because it does not contain a factor in the .5% column for an n of 144.

The HP-12C or the BA-II, however, can be used. Remember that n or N is 144 and i or %i is .5. The answer displayed will be \$42,240.18.

5. In this problem the annuity is a complex annuity. The value of c is 2 ÷ 4, or 1/2. Substituting in the formula for the PVA of a complex annuity, we have

$$= \left[\frac{1 - \left[\frac{1}{(1.08)^{10 \times 1/2}} \right]}{(1.08)^{1/2} - 1} \right] (\$500)$$

$$= \left[\frac{1 - .6806}{.0392} \right] (\$500)$$

$$= 8.1480 \times \$500$$

$$= \$4,074.00$$

APPENDIX A

TIME VALUE OF MONEY TABLES

TABLE A.1
FUTURE VALUE OF A SINGLE SUM

n \ i	0.5%	1.0%	1.5%	2.0%	2.5%	3.0%	3.5%	4.0%	4.5%
1	1.0050	1.0100	1.0150	1.0200	1.0250	1.0300	1.0350	1.0400	1.0450
2	1.0100	1.0201	1.0302	1.0404	1.0506	1.0609	1.0712	1.0816	1.0920
3	1.0151	1.0303	1.0457	1.0612	1.0769	1.0927	1.1087	1.1249	1.1412
4	1.0202	1.0406	1.0614	1.0824	1.1038	1.1255	1.1475	1.1699	1.1925
5	1.0253	1.0510	1.0773	1.1041	1.1314	1.1593	1.1877	1.2167	1.2462
6	1.0304	1.0615	1.0934	1.1262	1.1597	1.1941	1.2293	1.2653	1.3023
7	1.0355	1.0721	1.1098	1.1487	1.1887	1.2299	1.2723	1.3159	1.3609
8	1.0407	1.0829	1.1265	1.1717	1.2184	1.2668	1.3168	1.3686	1.4221
9	1.0459	1.0937	1.1434	1.1951	1.2489	1.3048	1.3629	1.4233	1.4861
10	1.0511	1.1046	1.1605	1.2190	1.2801	1.3439	1.4106	1.4802	1.5530
11	1.0564	1.1157	1.1779	1.2434	1.3121	1.3842	1.4600	1.5395	1.6229
12	1.0617	1.1268	1.1956	1.2682	1.3449	1.4258	1.5111	1.6010	1.6959
13	1.0670	1.1381	1.2136	1.2936	1.3785	1.4685	1.5640	1.6651	1.7722
14	1.0723	1.1495	1.2318	1.3195	1.4130	1.5126	1.6187	1.7317	1.8519
15	1.0777	1.1610	1.2502	1.3459	1.4483	1.5580	1.6753	1.8009	1.9353
16	1.0831	1.1726	1.2690	1.3728	1.4845	1.6047	1.7340	1.8730	2.0224
17	1.0885	1.1843	1.2880	1.4002	1.5216	1.6528	1.7947	1.9479	2.1134
18	1.0939	1.1961	1.3073	1.4282	1.5597	1.7024	1.8575	2.0258	2.2085
19	1.0994	1.2081	1.3270	1.4568	1.5987	1.7535	1.9225	2.1068	2.3079
20	1.1049	1.2202	1.3469	1.4859	1.6386	1.8061	1.9898	2.1911	2.4117
25	1.1328	1.2824	1.4509	1.6406	1.8539	2.0938	2.3632	2.6658	3.0054
30	1.1614	1.3478	1.5631	1.8114	2.0976	2.4273	2.8068	3.2434	3.7453
35	1.1907	1.4166	1.6839	1.9999	2.3732	2.8139	3.3336	3.9461	4.6673
40	1.2208	1.4889	1.8140	2.2080	2.6851	3.2620	3.9593	4.8010	5.8164
45	1.2516	1.5648	1.9542	2.4379	3.0379	3.7816	4.7024	5.8412	7.2482
50	1.2832	1.6446	2.1052	2.6916	3.4371	4.3839	5.5849	7.1067	9.0326

TABLE A.1 (CONT.)
FUTURE VALUE OF A SINGLE SUM

n \ i	5.0%	5.5%	6.0%	6.5%	7.0%	7.5%	8.0%	8.5%
1	1.0500	1.0550	1.0600	1.0650	1.0700	1.0750	1.0800	1.0850
2	1.1025	1.1130	1.1236	1.1342	1.1449	1.1556	1.1664	1.1772
3	1.1576	1.1742	1.1910	1.2079	1.2250	1.2423	1.2597	1.2773
4	1.2155	1.2388	1.2625	1.2865	1.3108	1.3355	1.3605	1.3859
5	1.2763	1.3070	1.3382	1.3701	1.4026	1.4356	1.4693	1.5037
6	1.3401	1.3788	1.4185	1.4591	1.5007	1.5433	1.5869	1.6315
7	1.4071	1.4547	1.5036	1.5540	1.6058	1.6590	1.7138	1.7701
8	1.4775	1.5347	1.5938	1.6550	1.7182	1.7835	1.8509	1.9206
9	1.5513	1.6191	1.6895	1.7626	1.8385	1.9172	1.9990	2.0839
10	1.6289	1.7081	1.7908	1.8771	1.9672	2.0610	2.1589	2.2610
11	1.7103	1.8021	1.8983	1.9992	2.1049	2.2156	2.3316	2.4532
12	1.7959	1.9012	2.0122	2.1291	2.2522	2.3818	2.5182	2.6617
13	1.8856	2.0058	2.1329	2.2675	2.4098	2.5604	2.7196	2.8879
14	1.9799	2.1161	2.2609	2.4149	2.5785	2.7524	2.9372	3.1334
15	2.0789	2.2325	2.3966	2.5718	2.7590	2.9589	3.1722	3.3997
16	2.1829	2.3553	2.5404	2.7390	2.9522	3.1808	3.4259	3.6887
17	2.2920	2.4848	2.6928	2.9170	3.1588	3.4194	3.7000	4.0023
18	2.4066	2.6215	2.8543	3.1067	3.3799	3.6758	3.9960	4.3425
19	2.5270	2.7656	3.0256	3.3086	3.6165	3.9515	4.3157	4.7116
20	2.6533	2.9178	3.2071	3.5236	3.8697	4.2479	4.6610	5.1120
25	3.3864	3.8134	4.2919	4.8277	5.4274	6.0983	6.8485	7.6868
30	4.3219	4.9840	5.7435	6.6144	7.6123	8.7550	10.0627	11.5583
35	5.5160	6.5138	7.6861	9.0623	10.6766	12.5689	14.7853	17.3796
40	7.0400	8.5133	10.2857	12.4161	14.9745	18.0442	21.7245	26.1330
45	8.9850	11.1266	13.7646	17.0111	21.0025	25.9048	31.9204	39.2951
50	11.4674	14.5420	18.4202	23.3067	29.4570	37.1897	46.9016	59.0863

A.3

TABLE A.1 (CONT.)
FUTURE VALUE OF A SINGLE SUM

n \ i	9.0%	9.5%	10.0%	10.5%	11.0%	11.5%	12.0%
1	1.0900	1.0950	1.1000	1.1050	1.1100	1.1150	1.1200
2	1.1881	1.1990	1.2100	1.2210	1.2321	1.2432	1.2544
3	1.2950	1.3129	1.3310	1.3492	1.3676	1.3862	1.4049
4	1.4116	1.4377	1.4641	1.4909	1.5181	1.5456	1.5735
5	1.5386	1.5742	1.6105	1.6474	1.6851	1.7234	1.7623
6	1.6771	1.7238	1.7716	1.8204	1.8704	1.9215	1.9738
7	1.8280	1.8876	1.9487	2.0116	2.0762	2.1425	2.2107
8	1.9926	2.0669	2.1436	2.2228	2.3045	2.3889	2.4760
9	2.1719	2.2632	2.3579	2.4562	2.5580	2.6636	2.7731
10	2.3674	2.4782	2.5937	2.7141	2.8394	2.9699	3.1058
11	2.5804	2.7137	2.8531	2.9991	3.1518	3.3115	3.4785
12	2.8127	2.9715	3.1384	3.3140	3.4985	3.6923	3.8960
13	3.0658	3.2537	3.4523	3.6619	3.8833	4.1169	4.3635
14	3.3417	3.5629	3.7975	4.0464	4.3104	4.5904	4.8871
15	3.6425	3.9013	4.1772	4.4713	4.7846	5.1183	5.4736
16	3.9703	4.2719	4.5950	4.9408	5.3109	5.7069	6.1304
17	4.3276	4.6778	5.0545	5.4596	5.8951	6.3632	6.8660
18	4.7171	5.1222	5.5599	6.0328	6.5436	7.0949	7.6900
19	5.1417	5.6088	6.1159	6.6663	7.2633	7.9108	8.6128
20	5.6044	6.1416	6.7275	7.3662	8.0623	8.8206	9.6463
25	8.6231	9.6684	10.8347	12.1355	13.5855	15.2010	17.0001
30	13.2677	15.2203	17.4494	19.9926	22.8923	26.1967	29.9599
35	20.4140	23.9604	28.1024	32.9367	38.5749	45.1461	52.7996
40	31.4094	37.7194	45.2593	54.2614	65.0009	77.8027	93.0510
45	48.3273	59.3793	72.8905	89.3928	109.5302	134.0816	163.9876
50	74.3575	93.4773	117.3909	147.2699	184.5648	231.0699	289.0022

A.4

TABLE A.1 (CONT.)
FUTURE VALUE OF A SINGLE SUM

n \ i	12.5%	13.0%	13.5%	14.0%	14.5%	15.0%	15.5%
1	1.1250	1.1300	1.1350	1.1400	1.1450	1.1500	1.1550
2	1.2656	1.2769	1.2882	1.2996	1.3110	1.3225	1.3340
3	1.4238	1.4429	1.4621	1.4815	1.5011	1.5209	1.5408
4	1.6018	1.6305	1.6595	1.6890	1.7188	1.7490	1.7796
5	1.8020	1.8424	1.8836	1.9254	1.9680	2.0114	2.0555
6	2.0273	2.0820	2.1378	2.1950	2.2534	2.3131	2.3741
7	2.2807	2.3526	2.4264	2.5023	2.5801	2.6600	2.7420
8	2.5658	2.6584	2.7540	2.8526	2.9542	3.0590	3.1671
9	2.8865	3.0040	3.1258	3.2519	3.3826	3.5179	3.6580
10	3.2473	3.3946	3.5478	3.7072	3.8731	4.0456	4.2249
11	3.6532	3.8359	4.0267	4.2262	4.4347	4.6524	4.8798
12	4.1099	4.3345	4.5704	4.8179	5.0777	5.3503	5.6362
13	4.6236	4.8980	5.1874	5.4924	5.8140	6.1528	6.5098
14	5.2016	5.5348	5.8877	6.2613	6.6570	7.0757	7.5188
15	5.8518	6.2543	6.6825	7.1379	7.6222	8.1371	8.6842
16	6.5833	7.0673	7.5846	8.1372	8.7275	9.3576	10.0302
17	7.4062	7.9861	8.6085	9.2765	9.9929	10.7613	11.5849
18	8.3319	9.0243	9.7707	10.5752	11.4419	12.3755	13.3806
19	9.3734	10.1974	11.0897	12.0557	13.1010	14.2318	15.4546
20	10.5451	11.5231	12.5869	13.7435	15.0006	16.3665	17.8501
25	19.0026	21.2305	23.7081	26.4619	29.5214	32.9190	36.6902
30	34.2433	39.1159	44.6556	50.9502	58.0985	66.2118	75.4153
35	61.7075	72.0685	84.1115	98.1002	114.3384	133.1755	155.0135
40	111.1990	132.7816	158.4289	188.8835	225.0191	267.8635	318.6246
45	200.3842	244.6414	298.4103	363.6791	442.8401	538.7693	654.9216
50	361.0989	450.7359	562.0735	700.2330	871.5139	1083.6574	1346.1678

TABLE A.1 (CONT.)
FUTURE VALUE OF A SINGLE SUM

n\i	16.0%	16.5%	17.0%	17.5%	18.0%	18.5%
1	1.1600	1.1650	1.1700	1.1750	1.1800	1.1850
2	1.3456	1.3572	1.3689	1.3806	1.3924	1.4042
3	1.5609	1.5812	1.6016	1.6222	1.6430	1.6640
4	1.8106	1.8421	1.8739	1.9061	1.9388	1.9718
5	2.1003	2.1460	2.1924	2.2397	2.2878	2.3366
6	2.4364	2.5001	2.5652	2.6316	2.6996	2.7689
7	2.8262	2.9126	3.0012	3.0922	3.1855	3.2812
8	3.2784	3.3932	3.5115	3.6333	3.7589	3.8882
9	3.8030	3.9531	4.1084	4.2691	4.4355	4.6075
10	4.4114	4.6053	4.8068	5.0162	5.2338	5.4599
11	5.1173	5.3652	5.6240	5.8941	6.1759	6.4700
12	5.9360	6.2504	6.5801	6.9256	7.2876	7.6669
13	6.8858	7.2818	7.6987	8.1375	8.5994	9.0853
14	7.9875	8.4833	9.0075	9.5616	10.1472	10.7661
15	9.2655	9.8830	10.5387	11.2349	11.9737	12.7578
16	10.7480	11.5137	12.3303	13.2010	14.1290	15.1180
17	12.4677	13.4135	14.4265	15.5111	16.6722	17.9148
18	14.4625	15.6267	16.8790	18.2256	19.6733	21.2290
19	16.7765	18.2051	19.7484	21.4151	23.2144	25.1564
20	19.4608	21.2089	23.1056	25.1627	27.3930	29.8103
25	40.8742	45.5143	50.6578	56.3568	62.6686	69.6560
30	85.8499	97.6737	111.0647	126.2223	143.3706	162.7611
35	180.3141	209.6078	243.5035	282.6997	327.9973	380.3140
40	378.7212	449.8182	533.8687	633.1617	750.3783	888.6567
45	795.4438	965.3096	1170.4794	1418.0907	1716.6839	2076.4705
50	1670.7038	2071.5540	2566.2153	3176.0939	3927.3569	4851.9634

n\i	19.0%	19.5%	20.0%	20.5%	21.0%	21.5%
1	1.1900	1.1950	1.2000	1.2050	1.2100	1.2150
2	1.4161	1.4280	1.4400	1.4520	1.4641	1.4762
3	1.6852	1.7065	1.7280	1.7497	1.7716	1.7936
4	2.0053	2.0393	2.0736	2.1084	2.1436	2.1792
5	2.3864	2.4369	2.4883	2.5406	2.5937	2.6478
6	2.8398	2.9121	2.9860	3.0614	3.1384	3.2170
7	3.3793	3.4800	3.5832	3.6890	3.7975	3.9087
8	4.0214	4.1586	4.2998	4.4453	4.5950	4.7491
9	4.7854	4.9695	5.1598	5.3565	5.5599	5.7701
10	5.6947	5.9385	6.1917	6.4546	6.7275	7.0107
11	6.7767	7.0965	7.4301	7.7778	8.1403	8.5180
12	8.0642	8.4804	8.9161	9.3723	9.8497	10.3494
13	9.5964	10.1340	10.6993	11.2936	11.9182	12.5745
14	11.4198	12.1102	12.8392	13.6088	14.4210	15.2780
15	13.5895	14.4717	15.4070	16.3986	17.4494	18.5628
16	16.1715	17.2936	18.4884	19.7603	21.1138	22.5538
17	19.2441	20.6659	22.1861	23.8111	25.5477	27.4029
18	22.9005	24.6958	26.6233	28.6924	30.9127	33.2945
19	27.2516	29.5114	31.9480	34.5743	37.4043	40.4529
20	32.4294	35.2662	38.3376	41.6621	45.2593	49.1502
25	77.3881	85.9405	95.3962	105.8464	117.3909	130.1388
30	184.6753	209.4292	237.3763	268.9128	304.4816	344.5786
35	440.7006	510.3601	590.6682	683.1981	789.7470	912.3673
40	1051.6675	1243.7017	1469.7716	1735.7288	2048.4002	2415.7452
45	2509.6506	3030.7892	3657.2620	4409.7819	5313.0226	6396.3542
50	5988.9139	7385.7612	9100.4382	11203.4646	13780.6123	16936.1190

TABLE A.1 (CONT.)
FUTURE VALUE OF A SINGLE SUM

n \ i	22.0%	22.5%	23.0%	23.5%	24.0%
1	1.2200	1.2250	1.2300	1.2350	1.2400
2	1.4884	1.5006	1.5129	1.5252	1.5376
3	1.8158	1.8383	1.8609	1.8837	1.9066
4	2.2153	2.2519	2.2889	2.3263	2.3642
5	2.7027	2.7585	2.8153	2.8730	2.9316
6	3.2973	3.3792	3.4628	3.5481	3.6352
7	4.0227	4.1395	4.2593	4.3820	4.5077
8	4.9077	5.0709	5.2389	5.4117	5.5895
9	5.9874	6.2119	6.4439	6.6835	6.9310
10	7.3046	7.6096	7.9259	8.2541	8.5944
11	8.9117	9.3217	9.7489	10.1938	10.6571
12	10.8722	11.4191	11.9912	12.5894	13.2148
13	13.2641	13.9884	14.7491	15.5479	16.3863
14	16.1822	17.1358	18.1414	19.2016	20.3191
15	19.7423	20.9914	22.3140	23.7140	25.1956
16	24.0856	25.7145	27.4462	29.2868	31.2426
17	29.3844	31.5002	33.7588	36.1691	38.7408
18	35.8490	38.5878	41.5233	44.6689	48.0386
19	43.7358	47.2700	51.0737	55.1661	59.5679
20	53.3576	57.9058	62.8206	68.1301	73.8641
25	144.2101	159.7358	176.8593	195.7375	216.5420
30	389.7579	440.6387	497.9129	562.3526	634.8199
35	1053.4018	1215.5228	1401.7769	1615.6360	1861.0540
40	2847.0378	3353.0772	3946.4305	4641.7132	5455.9126
45	7694.7122	9249.6221	11110.4082	13335.6163	15994.6902
50	20796.5615	25515.5207	31279.1953	38313.1518	46890.4346

```
TABLE A.1 (CONCLUDED)
FUTURE VALUE OF A SINGLE SUM
```

n \ i	24.5%	25.0%
1	1.2450	1.2500
2	1.5500	1.5625
3	1.9298	1.9531
4	2.4026	2.4414
5	2.9912	3.0518
6	3.7241	3.8147
7	4.6364	4.7684
8	5.7724	5.9605
9	7.1866	7.4506
10	8.9473	9.3132
11	11.1394	11.6415
12	13.8686	14.5519
13	17.2664	18.1899
14	21.4967	22.7374
15	26.7633	28.4217
16	33.3204	35.5271
17	41.4838	44.4089
18	51.6474	55.5112
19	64.3010	69.3889
20	80.0547	86.7362
25	239.4604	264.6978
30	716.2762	807.7936
35	2142.5319	2465.1903
40	6408.7607	7523.1638
45	19169.9427	22958.8740
50	57341.3049	70064.9232

TABLE A.2
PRESENT VALUE OF A SINGLE SUM

n \ i	0.5%	1.0%	1.5%	2.0%	2.5%	3.0%	3.5%	4.0%
1	0.9950	0.9901	0.9852	0.9804	0.9756	0.9709	0.9662	0.9615
2	0.9901	0.9803	0.9707	0.9612	0.9518	0.9426	0.9335	0.9246
3	0.9851	0.9706	0.9563	0.9423	0.9286	0.9151	0.9019	0.8890
4	0.9802	0.9610	0.9422	0.9238	0.9060	0.8885	0.8714	0.8548
5	0.9754	0.9515	0.9283	0.9057	0.8839	0.8626	0.8420	0.8219
6	0.9705	0.9420	0.9145	0.8880	0.8623	0.8375	0.8135	0.7903
7	0.9657	0.9327	0.9010	0.8706	0.8413	0.8131	0.7860	0.7599
8	0.9609	0.9235	0.8877	0.8535	0.8207	0.7894	0.7594	0.7307
9	0.9561	0.9143	0.8746	0.8368	0.8007	0.7664	0.7337	0.7026
10	0.9513	0.9053	0.8617	0.8203	0.7812	0.7441	0.7089	0.6756
11	0.9466	0.8963	0.8489	0.8043	0.7621	0.7224	0.6849	0.6496
12	0.9419	0.8874	0.8364	0.7885	0.7436	0.7014	0.6618	0.6246
13	0.9372	0.8787	0.8240	0.7730	0.7254	0.6810	0.6394	0.6006
14	0.9326	0.8700	0.8118	0.7579	0.7077	0.6611	0.6178	0.5775
15	0.9279	0.8613	0.7999	0.7430	0.6905	0.6419	0.5969	0.5553
16	0.9233	0.8528	0.7880	0.7284	0.6736	0.6232	0.5767	0.5339
17	0.9187	0.8444	0.7764	0.7142	0.6572	0.6050	0.5572	0.5134
18	0.9141	0.8360	0.7649	0.7002	0.6412	0.5874	0.5384	0.4936
19	0.9096	0.8277	0.7536	0.6864	0.6255	0.5703	0.5202	0.4746
20	0.9051	0.8195	0.7425	0.6730	0.6103	0.5537	0.5026	0.4564
25	0.8828	0.7798	0.6892	0.6095	0.5394	0.4776	0.4231	0.3751
30	0.8610	0.7419	0.6398	0.5521	0.4767	0.4120	0.3563	0.3083
35	0.8398	0.7059	0.5939	0.5000	0.4214	0.3554	0.3000	0.2534
40	0.8191	0.6717	0.5513	0.4529	0.3724	0.3066	0.2526	0.2083
45	0.7990	0.6391	0.5117	0.4102	0.3292	0.2644	0.2127	0.1712
50	0.7793	0.6080	0.4750	0.3715	0.2909	0.2281	0.1791	0.1407

TABLE A.2 (CONT.)
PRESENT VALUE OF A SINGLE SUM

n \ i	4.5%	5.0%	5.5%	6.0%	6.5%	7.0%	7.5%	8.0%
1	0.9569	0.9524	0.9479	0.9434	0.9390	0.9346	0.9302	0.9259
2	0.9157	0.9070	0.8985	0.8900	0.8817	0.8734	0.8653	0.8573
3	0.8763	0.8638	0.8516	0.8396	0.8278	0.8163	0.8050	0.7938
4	0.8386	0.8227	0.8072	0.7921	0.7773	0.7629	0.7488	0.7350
5	0.8025	0.7835	0.7651	0.7473	0.7299	0.7130	0.6966	0.6806
6	0.7679	0.7462	0.7252	0.7050	0.6853	0.6663	0.6480	0.6302
7	0.7348	0.7107	0.6874	0.6651	0.6435	0.6227	0.6028	0.5835
8	0.7032	0.6768	0.6516	0.6274	0.6042	0.5820	0.5607	0.5403
9	0.6729	0.6446	0.6176	0.5919	0.5674	0.5439	0.5216	0.5002
10	0.6439	0.6139	0.5854	0.5584	0.5327	0.5083	0.4852	0.4632
11	0.6162	0.5847	0.5549	0.5268	0.5002	0.4751	0.4513	0.4289
12	0.5897	0.5568	0.5260	0.4970	0.4697	0.4440	0.4199	0.3971
13	0.5643	0.5303	0.4986	0.4688	0.4410	0.4150	0.3906	0.3677
14	0.5400	0.5051	0.4726	0.4423	0.4141	0.3878	0.3633	0.3405
15	0.5167	0.4810	0.4479	0.4173	0.3888	0.3624	0.3380	0.3152
16	0.4945	0.4581	0.4246	0.3936	0.3651	0.3387	0.3144	0.2919
17	0.4732	0.4363	0.4024	0.3714	0.3428	0.3166	0.2925	0.2703
18	0.4528	0.4155	0.3815	0.3503	0.3219	0.2959	0.2720	0.2502
19	0.4333	0.3957	0.3616	0.3305	0.3022	0.2765	0.2531	0.2317
20	0.4146	0.3769	0.3427	0.3118	0.2838	0.2584	0.2354	0.2145
25	0.3327	0.2953	0.2622	0.2330	0.2071	0.1842	0.1640	0.1460
30	0.2670	0.2314	0.2006	0.1741	0.1512	0.1314	0.1142	0.0994
35	0.2143	0.1813	0.1535	0.1301	0.1103	0.0937	0.0796	0.0676
40	0.1719	0.1420	0.1175	0.0972	0.0805	0.0668	0.0554	0.0460
45	0.1380	0.1113	0.0899	0.0727	0.0588	0.0476	0.0386	0.0313
50	0.1107	0.0872	0.0688	0.0543	0.0429	0.0339	0.0269	0.0213

TABLE A.2 (CONT.)
PRESENT VALUE OF A SINGLE SUM

n \ i	8.5%	9.0%	9.5%	10.0%	10.5%	11.0%	11.5%	12.0%
1	0.9217	0.9174	0.9132	0.9091	0.9050	0.9009	0.8969	0.8929
2	0.8495	0.8417	0.8340	0.8264	0.8190	0.8116	0.8044	0.7972
3	0.7829	0.7722	0.7617	0.7513	0.7412	0.7312	0.7214	0.7118
4	0.7216	0.7084	0.6956	0.6830	0.6707	0.6587	0.6470	0.6355
5	0.6650	0.6499	0.6352	0.6209	0.6070	0.5935	0.5803	0.5674
6	0.6129	0.5963	0.5801	0.5645	0.5493	0.5346	0.5204	0.5066
7	0.5649	0.5470	0.5298	0.5132	0.4971	0.4817	0.4667	0.4523
8	0.5207	0.5019	0.4838	0.4665	0.4499	0.4339	0.4186	0.4039
9	0.4799	0.4604	0.4418	0.4241	0.4071	0.3909	0.3754	0.3606
10	0.4423	0.4224	0.4035	0.3855	0.3684	0.3522	0.3367	0.3220
11	0.4076	0.3875	0.3685	0.3505	0.3334	0.3173	0.3020	0.2875
12	0.3757	0.3555	0.3365	0.3186	0.3018	0.2858	0.2708	0.2567
13	0.3463	0.3262	0.3073	0.2897	0.2731	0.2575	0.2429	0.2292
14	0.3191	0.2992	0.2807	0.2633	0.2471	0.2320	0.2178	0.2046
15	0.2941	0.2745	0.2563	0.2394	0.2236	0.2090	0.1954	0.1827
16	0.2711	0.2519	0.2341	0.2176	0.2024	0.1883	0.1752	0.1631
17	0.2499	0.2311	0.2138	0.1978	0.1832	0.1696	0.1572	0.1456
18	0.2303	0.2120	0.1952	0.1799	0.1658	0.1528	0.1409	0.1300
19	0.2122	0.1945	0.1783	0.1635	0.1500	0.1377	0.1264	0.1161
20	0.1956	0.1784	0.1628	0.1486	0.1358	0.1240	0.1134	0.1037
25	0.1301	0.1160	0.1034	0.0923	0.0824	0.0736	0.0658	0.0588
30	0.0865	0.0754	0.0657	0.0573	0.0500	0.0437	0.0382	0.0334
35	0.0575	0.0490	0.0417	0.0356	0.0304	0.0259	0.0222	0.0189
40	0.0383	0.0318	0.0265	0.0221	0.0184	0.0154	0.0129	0.0107
45	0.0254	0.0207	0.0168	0.0137	0.0112	0.0091	0.0075	0.0061
50	0.0169	0.0134	0.0107	0.0085	0.0068	0.0054	0.0043	0.0035

TABLE A.2 (CONT.)
PRESENT VALUE OF A SINGLE SUM

n\i	12.5%	13.0%	13.5%	14.0%	14.5%	15.0%	15.5%	16.0%
1	0.8889	0.8850	0.8811	0.8772	0.8734	0.8696	0.8658	0.8621
2	0.7901	0.7831	0.7763	0.7695	0.7628	0.7561	0.7496	0.7432
3	0.7023	0.6931	0.6839	0.6750	0.6662	0.6575	0.6490	0.6407
4	0.6243	0.6133	0.6026	0.5921	0.5818	0.5718	0.5619	0.5523
5	0.5549	0.5428	0.5309	0.5194	0.5081	0.4972	0.4865	0.4761
6	0.4933	0.4803	0.4678	0.4556	0.4438	0.4323	0.4212	0.4104
7	0.4385	0.4251	0.4121	0.3996	0.3876	0.3759	0.3647	0.3538
8	0.3897	0.3762	0.3631	0.3506	0.3385	0.3269	0.3158	0.3050
9	0.3464	0.3329	0.3199	0.3075	0.2956	0.2843	0.2734	0.2630
10	0.3079	0.2946	0.2819	0.2697	0.2582	0.2472	0.2367	0.2267
11	0.2737	0.2607	0.2483	0.2366	0.2255	0.2149	0.2049	0.1954
12	0.2433	0.2307	0.2188	0.2076	0.1969	0.1869	0.1774	0.1685
13	0.2163	0.2042	0.1928	0.1821	0.1720	0.1625	0.1536	0.1452
14	0.1922	0.1807	0.1698	0.1597	0.1502	0.1413	0.1330	0.1252
15	0.1709	0.1599	0.1496	0.1401	0.1312	0.1229	0.1152	0.1079
16	0.1519	0.1415	0.1318	0.1229	0.1146	0.1069	0.0997	0.0930
17	0.1350	0.1252	0.1162	0.1078	0.1001	0.0929	0.0863	0.0802
18	0.1200	0.1108	0.1023	0.0946	0.0874	0.0808	0.0747	0.0691
19	0.1067	0.0981	0.0902	0.0829	0.0763	0.0703	0.0647	0.0596
20	0.0948	0.0868	0.0794	0.0728	0.0667	0.0611	0.0560	0.0514
25	0.0526	0.0471	0.0422	0.0378	0.0339	0.0304	0.0273	0.0245
30	0.0292	0.0256	0.0224	0.0196	0.0172	0.0151	0.0133	0.0116
35	0.0162	0.0139	0.0119	0.0102	0.0087	0.0075	0.0065	0.0055
40	0.0090	0.0075	0.0063	0.0053	0.0044	0.0037	0.0031	0.0026
45	0.0050	0.0041	0.0034	0.0027	0.0023	0.0019	0.0015	0.0013
50	0.0028	0.0022	0.0018	0.0014	0.0011	0.0009	0.0007	0.0006

TABLE A.2 (CONT.)
PRESENT VALUE OF A SINGLE SUM

n\i	16.5%	17.0%	17.5%	18.0%	18.5%	19.0%	19.5%
1	0.8584	0.8547	0.8511	0.8475	0.8439	0.8403	0.8368
2	0.7368	0.7305	0.7243	0.7182	0.7121	0.7062	0.7003
3	0.6324	0.6244	0.6164	0.6086	0.6010	0.5934	0.5860
4	0.5429	0.5337	0.5246	0.5158	0.5071	0.4987	0.4904
5	0.4660	0.4561	0.4465	0.4371	0.4280	0.4190	0.4104
6	0.4000	0.3898	0.3800	0.3704	0.3612	0.3521	0.3434
7	0.3433	0.3332	0.3234	0.3139	0.3048	0.2959	0.2874
8	0.2947	0.2848	0.2752	0.2660	0.2572	0.2487	0.2405
9	0.2530	0.2434	0.2342	0.2255	0.2170	0.2090	0.2012
10	0.2171	0.2080	0.1994	0.1911	0.1832	0.1756	0.1684
11	0.1864	0.1778	0.1697	0.1619	0.1546	0.1476	0.1409
12	0.1600	0.1520	0.1444	0.1372	0.1304	0.1240	0.1179
13	0.1373	0.1299	0.1229	0.1163	0.1101	0.1042	0.0987
14	0.1179	0.1110	0.1046	0.0985	0.0929	0.0876	0.0826
15	0.1012	0.0949	0.0890	0.0835	0.0784	0.0736	0.0691
16	0.0869	0.0811	0.0758	0.0708	0.0661	0.0618	0.0578
17	0.0746	0.0693	0.0645	0.0600	0.0558	0.0520	0.0484
18	0.0640	0.0592	0.0549	0.0508	0.0471	0.0437	0.0405
19	0.0549	0.0506	0.0467	0.0431	0.0398	0.0367	0.0339
20	0.0471	0.0433	0.0397	0.0365	0.0335	0.0308	0.0284
25	0.0220	0.0197	0.0177	0.0160	0.0144	0.0129	0.0116
30	0.0102	0.0090	0.0079	0.0070	0.0061	0.0054	0.0048
35	0.0048	0.0041	0.0035	0.0030	0.0026	0.0023	0.0020
40	0.0022	0.0019	0.0016	0.0013	0.0011	0.0010	0.0008
45	0.0010	0.0009	0.0007	0.0006	0.0005	0.0004	0.0003
50	0.0005	0.0004	0.0003	0.000255	0.000206	0.000167	0.000135

TABLE A.2 (CONT.)
PRESENT VALUE OF A SINGLE SUM

n \ i	20.0%	20.5%	21.0%	21.5%	22.0%	22.5%	23.0%
1	0.8333	0.8299	0.8264	0.8230	0.8197	0.8163	0.8130
2	0.6944	0.6887	0.6830	0.6774	0.6719	0.6664	0.6610
3	0.5787	0.5715	0.5645	0.5575	0.5507	0.5440	0.5374
4	0.4823	0.4743	0.4665	0.4589	0.4514	0.4441	0.4369
5	0.4019	0.3936	0.3855	0.3777	0.3700	0.3625	0.3552
6	0.3349	0.3266	0.3186	0.3108	0.3033	0.2959	0.2888
7	0.2791	0.2711	0.2633	0.2558	0.2486	0.2416	0.2348
8	0.2326	0.2250	0.2176	0.2106	0.2038	0.1972	0.1909
9	0.1938	0.1867	0.1799	0.1733	0.1670	0.1610	0.1552
10	0.1615	0.1549	0.1486	0.1426	0.1369	0.1314	0.1262
11	0.1346	0.1286	0.1228	0.1174	0.1122	0.1073	0.1026
12	0.1122	0.1067	0.1015	0.0966	0.0920	0.0876	0.0834
13	0.0935	0.0885	0.0839	0.0795	0.0754	0.0715	0.0678
14	0.0779	0.0735	0.0693	0.0655	0.0618	0.0584	0.0551
15	0.0649	0.0610	0.0573	0.0539	0.0507	0.0476	0.0448
16	0.0541	0.0506	0.0474	0.0443	0.0415	0.0389	0.0364
17	0.0451	0.0420	0.0391	0.0365	0.0340	0.0317	0.0296
18	0.0376	0.0349	0.0323	0.0300	0.0279	0.0259	0.0241
19	0.0313	0.0289	0.0267	0.0247	0.0229	0.0212	0.0196
20	0.0261	0.0240	0.0221	0.0203	0.0187	0.0173	0.0159
25	0.0105	0.0094	0.0085	0.0077	0.0069	0.0063	0.0057
30	0.0042	0.0037	0.0033	0.0029	0.0026	0.0023	0.0020
35	0.0017	0.0015	0.0013	0.0011	0.0009	0.0008	0.0007
40	0.0007	0.0006	0.0005	0.0004	0.000351	0.000298	0.000253
45	0.000273	0.000227	0.000188	0.000156	0.000130	0.000108	0.000090
50	0.000110	0.000089	0.000073	0.000059	0.000048	0.000039	0.000032

TABLE A.2 (CONCLUDED)
PRESENT VALUE OF A SINGLE SUM

n \ i	23.5%	24.0%	24.5%	25.0%
1	0.8097	0.8065	0.8032	0.8000
2	0.6556	0.6504	0.6452	0.6400
3	0.5309	0.5245	0.5182	0.5120
4	0.4299	0.4230	0.4162	0.4096
5	0.3481	0.3411	0.3343	0.3277
6	0.2818	0.2751	0.2685	0.2621
7	0.2282	0.2218	0.2157	0.2097
8	0.1848	0.1789	0.1732	0.1678
9	0.1496	0.1443	0.1391	0.1342
10	0.1212	0.1164	0.1118	0.1074
11	0.0981	0.0938	0.0898	0.0859
12	0.0794	0.0757	0.0721	0.0687
13	0.0643	0.0610	0.0579	0.0550
14	0.0521	0.0492	0.0465	0.0440
15	0.0422	0.0397	0.0374	0.0352
16	0.0341	0.0320	0.0300	0.0281
17	0.0276	0.0258	0.0241	0.0225
18	0.0224	0.0208	0.0194	0.0180
19	0.0181	0.0168	0.0156	0.0144
20	0.0147	0.0135	0.0125	0.0115
25	0.0051	0.0046	0.0042	0.0038
30	0.0018	0.0016	0.0014	0.0012
35	0.0006	0.0005	0.000467	0.000406
40	0.000215	0.000183	0.000156	0.000133
45	0.000075	0.000063	0.000052	0.000044
50	0.000026	0.000021	0.000017	0.000014

TABLE A.3
FUTURE VALUE OF AN ANNUITY

n\i	0.5%	1.0%	1.5%	2.0%	2.5%	3.0%	3.5%
1	1.0000	1.0000	1.0000	1.0000	1.0000	1.0000	1.0000
2	2.0050	2.0100	2.0150	2.0200	2.0250	2.0300	2.0350
3	3.0150	3.0301	3.0452	3.0604	3.0756	3.0909	3.1062
4	4.0301	4.0604	4.0909	4.1216	4.1525	4.1836	4.2149
5	5.0503	5.1010	5.1523	5.2040	5.2563	5.3091	5.3625
6	6.0755	6.1520	6.2296	6.3081	6.3877	6.4684	6.5502
7	7.1059	7.2135	7.3230	7.4343	7.5474	7.6625	7.7794
8	8.1414	8.2857	8.4328	8.5830	8.7361	8.8923	9.0517
9	9.1821	9.3685	9.5593	9.7546	9.9545	10.1591	10.3685
10	10.2280	10.4622	10.7027	10.9497	11.2034	11.4639	11.7314
11	11.2792	11.5668	11.8633	12.1687	12.4835	12.8078	13.1420
12	12.3356	12.6825	13.0412	13.4121	13.7956	14.1920	14.6020
13	13.3972	13.8093	14.2368	14.6803	15.1404	15.6178	16.1130
14	14.4642	14.9474	15.4504	15.9739	16.5190	17.0863	17.6770
15	15.5365	16.0969	16.6821	17.2934	17.9319	18.5989	19.2957
16	16.6142	17.2579	17.9324	18.6393	19.3802	20.1569	20.9710
17	17.6973	18.4304	19.2014	20.0121	20.8647	21.7616	22.7050
18	18.7858	19.6147	20.4894	21.4123	22.3863	23.4144	24.4997
19	19.8797	20.8109	21.7967	22.8406	23.9460	25.1169	26.3572
20	20.9791	22.0190	23.1237	24.2974	25.5447	26.8704	28.2797
25	26.5591	28.2432	30.0630	32.0303	34.1578	36.4593	38.9499
30	32.2800	34.7849	37.5387	40.5681	43.9027	47.5754	51.6227
35	38.1454	41.6603	45.5921	49.9945	54.9282	60.4621	66.6740
40	44.1588	48.8864	54.2679	60.4020	67.4026	75.4013	84.5503
45	50.3242	56.4811	63.6142	71.8927	81.5161	92.7199	105.7817
50	56.6452	64.4632	73.6828	84.5794	97.4843	112.7969	130.9979

TABLE A.3 (CONT.)
FUTURE VALUE OF AN ANNUITY

n\i	4.0%	4.5%	5.0%	5.5%	6.0%	6.5%
1	1.0000	1.0000	1.0000	1.0000	1.0000	1.0000
2	2.0400	2.0450	2.0500	2.0550	2.0600	2.0650
3	3.1216	3.1370	3.1525	3.1680	3.1836	3.1992
4	4.2465	4.2782	4.3101	4.3423	4.3746	4.4072
5	5.4163	5.4707	5.5256	5.5811	5.6371	5.6936
6	6.6330	6.7169	6.8019	6.8881	6.9753	7.0637
7	7.8983	8.0192	8.1420	8.2669	8.3938	8.5229
8	9.2142	9.3800	9.5491	9.7216	9.8975	10.0769
9	10.5828	10.8021	11.0266	11.2563	11.4913	11.7319
10	12.0061	12.2882	12.5779	12.8754	13.1808	13.4944
11	13.4864	13.8412	14.2068	14.5835	14.9716	15.3716
12	15.0258	15.4640	15.9171	16.3856	16.8699	17.3707
13	16.6268	17.1599	17.7130	18.2868	18.8821	19.4998
14	18.2919	18.9321	19.5986	20.2926	21.0151	21.7673
15	20.0236	20.7841	21.5786	22.4087	23.2760	24.1822
16	21.8245	22.7193	23.6575	24.6411	25.6725	26.7540
17	23.6975	24.7417	25.8404	26.9964	28.2129	29.4930
18	25.6454	26.8551	28.1324	29.4812	30.9057	32.4101
19	27.6712	29.0636	30.5390	32.1027	33.7600	35.5167
20	29.7781	31.3714	33.0660	34.8683	36.7856	38.8253
25	41.6459	44.5652	47.7271	51.1526	54.8645	58.8877
30	56.0849	61.0071	66.4388	72.4355	79.0582	86.3749
35	73.6522	81.4966	90.3203	100.2514	111.4348	124.0347
40	95.0255	107.0303	120.7998	136.6056	154.7620	175.6319
45	121.0294	138.8500	159.7002	184.1192	212.7435	246.3246
50	152.6671	178.5030	209.3480	246.2175	290.3359	343.1797

TABLE A.3 (CONT.)
FUTURE VALUE OF AN ANNUITY

n\i	7.0%	7.5%	8.0%	8.5%	9.0%	9.5%
1	1.0000	1.0000	1.0000	1.0000	1.0000	1.0000
2	2.0700	2.0750	2.0800	2.0850	2.0900	2.0950
3	3.2149	3.2306	3.2464	3.2622	3.2781	3.2940
4	4.4399	4.4729	4.5061	4.5395	4.5731	4.6070
5	5.7507	5.8084	5.8666	5.9254	5.9847	6.0446
6	7.1533	7.2440	7.3359	7.4290	7.5233	7.6189
7	8.6540	8.7873	8.9228	9.0605	9.2004	9.3426
8	10.2598	10.4464	10.6366	10.8306	11.0285	11.2302
9	11.9780	12.2298	12.4876	12.7512	13.0210	13.2971
10	13.8164	14.1471	14.4866	14.8351	15.1929	15.5603
11	15.7836	16.2081	16.6455	17.0961	17.5603	18.0385
12	17.8885	18.4237	18.9771	19.5492	20.1407	20.7522
13	20.1406	20.8055	21.4953	22.2109	22.9534	23.7236
14	22.5505	23.3659	24.2149	25.0989	26.0192	26.9774
15	25.1290	26.1184	27.1521	28.2323	29.3609	30.5402
16	27.8881	29.0772	30.3243	31.6320	33.0034	34.4416
17	30.8402	32.2580	33.7502	35.3207	36.9737	38.7135
18	33.9990	35.6774	37.4502	39.3230	41.3013	43.3913
19	37.3790	39.3532	41.4463	43.6654	46.0185	48.5135
20	40.9955	43.3047	45.7620	48.3770	51.1601	54.1222
25	63.2490	67.9779	73.1059	78.6678	84.7009	91.2459
30	94.4608	103.3994	113.2832	124.2147	136.3075	149.6875
35	138.2369	154.2516	172.3168	192.7017	215.7108	241.6885
40	199.6351	227.2565	259.0565	295.6825	337.8824	386.5200
45	285.7493	332.0645	386.5056	450.5304	525.8587	614.5194
50	406.5289	482.5299	573.7702	683.3684	815.0836	973.4448

TABLE A.3 (CONT.)
FUTURE VALUE OF AN ANNUITY

n\i	10.0%	10.5%	11.0%	11.5%	12.0%	12.5%
1	1.0000	1.0000	1.0000	1.0000	1.0000	1.0000
2	2.1000	2.1050	2.1100	2.1150	2.1200	2.1250
3	3.3100	3.3260	3.3421	3.3582	3.3744	3.3906
4	4.6410	4.6753	4.7097	4.7444	4.7793	4.8145
5	6.1051	6.1662	6.2278	6.2900	6.3528	6.4163
6	7.7156	7.8136	7.9129	8.0134	8.1152	8.2183
7	9.4872	9.6340	9.7833	9.9349	10.0890	10.2456
8	11.4359	11.6456	11.8594	12.0774	12.2997	12.5263
9	13.5795	13.8684	14.1640	14.4663	14.7757	15.0921
10	15.9374	16.3246	16.7220	17.1300	17.5487	17.9786
11	18.5312	19.0387	19.5614	20.0999	20.6546	21.2259
12	21.3843	22.0377	22.7132	23.4114	24.1331	24.8791
13	24.5227	25.3517	26.2116	27.1037	28.0291	28.9890
14	27.9750	29.0136	30.0949	31.2207	32.3926	33.6126
15	31.7725	33.0600	34.4054	35.8110	37.2797	38.8142
16	35.9497	37.5313	39.1899	40.9293	42.7533	44.6660
17	40.5447	42.4721	44.5008	46.6362	48.8837	51.2493
18	45.5992	47.9317	50.3959	52.9993	55.7497	58.6554
19	51.1591	53.9645	56.9395	60.0942	63.4397	66.9873
20	57.2750	60.6308	64.2028	68.0051	72.0524	76.3608
25	98.3471	106.0522	114.4133	123.4868	133.3339	144.0208
30	164.4940	180.8815	199.0209	219.1014	241.3327	265.9464
35	271.0244	304.1588	341.5896	383.8792	431.6635	485.6604
40	442.5926	507.2516	581.8261	667.8496	767.0914	881.5920
45	718.9048	841.8361	986.6386	1157.2309	1358.2300	1595.0737
50	1163.9085	1393.0464	1668.7712	2000.6078	2400.0182	2880.7909

TABLE A.3 (CONT.)
FUTURE VALUE OF AN ANNUITY

n \ i	13.0%	13.5%	14.0%	14.5%	15.0%	15.5%
1	1.0000	1.0000	1.0000	1.0000	1.0000	1.0000
2	2.1300	2.1350	2.1400	2.1450	2.1500	2.1550
3	3.4069	3.4232	3.4396	3.4560	3.4725	3.4890
4	4.8498	4.8854	4.9211	4.9571	4.9934	5.0298
5	6.4803	6.5449	6.6101	6.6759	6.7424	6.8094
6	8.3227	8.4284	8.5355	8.6439	8.7537	8.8649
7	10.4047	10.5663	10.7305	10.8973	11.0668	11.2390
8	12.7573	12.9927	13.2328	13.4774	13.7268	13.9810
9	15.4157	15.7468	16.0853	16.4317	16.7858	17.1481
10	18.4197	18.8726	19.3373	19.8142	20.3037	20.8060
11	21.8143	22.4204	23.0445	23.6873	24.3493	25.0310
12	25.6502	26.4471	27.2707	28.1220	29.0017	29.9108
13	29.9847	31.0175	32.0887	33.1997	34.3519	35.5469
14	34.8827	36.2048	37.5811	39.0136	40.5047	42.0567
15	40.4175	42.0925	43.8424	45.6706	47.5804	49.5755
16	46.6717	48.7750	50.9804	53.2928	55.7175	58.2597
17	53.7391	56.3596	59.1176	62.0203	65.0751	68.2899
18	61.7251	64.9681	68.3941	72.0132	75.8364	79.8749
19	70.7494	74.7388	78.9692	83.4551	88.2118	93.2555
20	80.9468	85.8286	91.0249	96.5561	102.4436	108.7101
25	155.6196	168.2081	181.8708	196.6994	212.7930	230.2591
30	293.1992	323.3748	356.7868	393.7825	434.7451	480.0988
35	546.6808	615.6404	693.5727	781.6440	881.1702	993.6353
40	1013.7042	1166.1401	1342.0251	1544.9596	1779.0903	2049.1913
45	1874.1646	2203.0391	2590.5648	3047.1728	3585.1285	4218.8488
50	3459.5071	4156.0997	4994.5213	6003.5444	7217.7163	8678.5022

TABLE A.3 (CONT.)
FUTURE VALUE OF AN ANNUITY

n \ i	16.0%	16.5%	17.0%	17.5%	18.0%
1	1.0000	1.0000	1.0000	1.0000	1.0000
2	2.1600	2.1650	2.1700	2.1750	2.1800
3	3.5056	3.5222	3.5389	3.5556	3.5724
4	5.0665	5.1034	5.1405	5.1779	5.2154
5	6.8771	6.9455	7.0144	7.0840	7.1542
6	8.9775	9.0915	9.2068	9.3237	9.4420
7	11.4139	11.5915	11.7720	11.9553	12.1415
8	14.2401	14.5041	14.7733	15.0475	15.3270
9	17.5185	17.8973	18.2847	18.6808	19.0859
10	21.3215	21.8504	22.3931	22.9500	23.5213
11	25.7329	26.4557	27.1999	27.9662	28.7551
12	30.8502	31.8209	32.8239	33.8603	34.9311
13	36.7862	38.0713	39.4040	40.7858	42.2187
14	43.6720	45.3531	47.1027	48.9234	50.8180
15	51.6595	53.8364	56.1101	58.4850	60.9653
16	60.9250	63.7194	66.6488	69.7198	72.9390
17	71.6730	75.2331	78.9792	82.9208	87.0680
18	84.1407	88.6465	93.4056	98.4319	103.7403
19	98.6032	104.2732	110.2846	116.6575	123.4135
20	115.3797	122.4783	130.0329	138.0726	146.6280
25	249.2140	269.7838	292.1049	316.3248	342.6035
30	530.3117	585.9014	647.4391	715.5558	790.9480
35	1120.7130	1264.2895	1426.4910	1609.7125	1816.6516
40	2360.7572	2720.1102	3134.5218	3612.3528	4163.2130
45	4965.2739	5844.3008	6879.2907	8097.6609	9531.5771
50	10435.6488	12548.8124	15089.5017	18143.3936	21813.0937

TABLE A.3 (CONT.)
FUTURE VALUE OF AN ANNUITY

n \ i	18.5%	19.0%	19.5%	20.0%	20.5%
1	1.0000	1.0000	1.0000	1.0000	1.0000
2	2.1850	2.1900	2.1950	2.2000	2.2050
3	3.5892	3.6061	3.6230	3.6400	3.6570
4	5.2532	5.2913	5.3295	5.3680	5.4067
5	7.2251	7.2966	7.3688	7.4416	7.5151
6	9.5617	9.6830	9.8057	9.9299	10.0557
7	12.3306	12.5227	12.7178	12.9159	13.1171
8	15.6118	15.9020	16.1978	16.4991	16.8061
9	19.5000	19.9234	20.3563	20.7989	21.2514
10	24.1075	24.7089	25.3258	25.9587	26.6079
11	29.5674	30.4035	31.2643	32.1504	33.0625
12	36.0373	37.1802	38.3609	39.5805	40.8403
13	43.7042	45.2445	46.8412	48.4966	50.2126
14	52.7895	54.8409	56.9753	59.1959	61.5062
15	63.5556	66.2607	69.0855	72.0351	75.1149
16	76.3134	79.8502	83.5571	87.4421	91.5135
17	91.4313	96.0218	100.8508	105.9306	111.2737
18	109.3461	115.2659	121.5167	128.1167	135.0849
19	130.5752	138.1664	146.2124	154.7400	163.7773
20	155.7316	165.4180	175.7239	186.6880	198.3516
25	371.1137	402.0425	435.5921	471.9811	511.4460
30	874.3841	966.7122	1068.8675	1181.8816	1306.8915
35	2050.3457	2314.2137	2612.1029	2948.3411	3327.7955
40	4798.1443	5529.8290	6372.8290	7343.8578	8462.0918
45	11218.7595	13203.4242	15537.3808	18281.3099	21506.2532
50	26221.4239	31515.3363	37870.5705	45497.1908	54646.1687

TABLE A.3 (CONT.)
FUTURE VALUE OF AN ANNUITY

n \ i	21.0%	21.5%	22.0%	22.5%	23.0%
1	1.0000	1.0000	1.0000	1.0000	1.0000
2	2.2100	2.2150	2.2200	2.2250	2.2300
3	3.6741	3.6912	3.7084	3.7256	3.7429
4	5.4457	5.4848	5.5242	5.5639	5.6038
5	7.5892	7.6641	7.7396	7.8158	7.8926
6	10.1830	10.3119	10.4423	10.5743	10.7079
7	13.3214	13.5289	13.7396	13.9535	14.1708
8	17.1189	17.4376	17.7623	18.0931	18.4300
9	21.7139	22.1867	22.6700	23.1640	23.6690
10	27.2738	27.9568	28.6574	29.3759	30.1128
11	34.0013	34.9676	35.9620	36.9855	38.0388
12	42.1416	43.4856	44.8737	46.3072	47.7877
13	51.9913	53.8350	55.7459	57.7264	59.7788
14	63.9095	66.4095	69.0100	71.7148	74.5280
15	78.3305	81.6876	85.1922	88.8507	92.6694
16	95.7799	100.2504	104.9345	109.8420	114.9834
17	116.8937	122.8042	129.0201	135.5565	142.4295
18	142.4413	150.2072	158.4045	167.0567	176.1883
19	173.3540	183.5017	194.2535	205.6445	217.7116
20	210.7584	223.9546	237.9893	252.9145	268.7853
25	554.2422	600.6458	650.9551	705.4924	764.6054
30	1445.1507	1598.0401	1767.0813	1953.9499	2160.4907
35	3755.9379	4238.9178	4783.6447	5397.8790	6090.3344
40	9749.5248	11231.3728	12936.5353	14898.1207	17154.0456
45	25295.3458	29745.8336	34971.4191	41104.9873	48301.7747
50	65617.2016	78767.9954	94525.2793	113397.8697	135992.1536

TABLE A.3 (CONCLUDED)
FUTURE VALUE OF AN ANNUITY

n \ i	23.5%	24.0%	24.5%	25.0%
1	1.0000	1.0000	1.0000	1.0000
2	2.2350	2.2400	2.2450	2.2500
3	3.7602	3.7776	3.7950	3.8125
4	5.6439	5.6842	5.7248	5.7656
5	7.9702	8.0484	8.1274	8.2070
6	10.8432	10.9801	11.1186	11.2588
7	14.3913	14.6153	14.8426	15.0735
8	18.7733	19.1229	19.4791	19.8419
9	24.1850	24.7125	25.2515	25.8023
10	30.8685	31.6434	32.4381	33.2529
11	39.1226	40.2379	41.3854	42.5661
12	49.3164	50.8950	52.5248	54.2077
13	61.9058	64.1097	66.3934	68.7596
14	77.4536	80.4961	83.6598	86.9495
15	96.6552	100.8151	105.1565	109.6868
16	120.3692	126.0108	131.9198	138.1085
17	149.6559	157.2534	165.2402	173.6357
18	185.8251	195.9942	206.7240	218.0446
19	230.4940	244.0328	258.3714	273.5558
20	285.6601	303.6006	322.6724	342.9447
25	828.6700	898.0916	973.3079	1054.7912
30	2388.7346	2640.9164	2919.4948	3227.1743
35	6870.7914	7750.2251	8740.9466	9856.7613
40	19747.7158	22728.8026	26154.1254	30088.6554
45	56743.0482	66640.3758	78240.5824	91831.4962
50	163030.4330	195372.6442	234042.0607	280255.6929

TABLE A.4
PRESENT VALUE OF AN ANNUITY

n \ i	0.5%	1.0%	1.5%	2.0%	2.5%	3.0%	3.5%
1	0.9950	0.9901	0.9852	0.9804	0.9756	0.9709	0.9662
2	1.9851	1.9704	1.9559	1.9416	1.9274	1.9135	1.8997
3	2.9702	2.9410	2.9122	2.8839	2.8560	2.8286	2.8016
4	3.9505	3.9020	3.8544	3.8077	3.7620	3.7171	3.6731
5	4.9259	4.8534	4.7826	4.7135	4.6458	4.5797	4.5151
6	5.8964	5.7955	5.6972	5.6014	5.5081	5.4172	5.3286
7	6.8621	6.7282	6.5982	6.4720	6.3494	6.2303	6.1145
8	7.8230	7.6517	7.4859	7.3255	7.1701	7.0197	6.8740
9	8.7791	8.5660	8.3605	8.1622	7.9709	7.7861	7.6077
10	9.7304	9.4713	9.2222	8.9826	8.7521	8.5302	8.3166
11	10.6770	10.3676	10.0711	9.7868	9.5142	9.2526	9.0016
12	11.6189	11.2551	10.9075	10.5753	10.2578	9.9540	9.6633
13	12.5562	12.1337	11.7315	11.3484	10.9832	10.6350	10.3027
14	13.4887	13.0037	12.5434	12.1062	11.6909	11.2961	10.9205
15	14.4166	13.8651	13.3432	12.8493	12.3814	11.9379	11.5174
16	15.3399	14.7179	14.1313	13.5777	13.0550	12.5611	12.0941
17	16.2586	15.5623	14.9076	14.2919	13.7122	13.1661	12.6513
18	17.1728	16.3983	15.6726	14.9920	14.3534	13.7535	13.1897
19	18.0824	17.2260	16.4262	15.6785	14.9789	14.3238	13.7098
20	18.9874	18.0456	17.1686	16.3514	15.5892	14.8775	14.2124
25	23.4456	22.0232	20.7196	19.5235	18.4244	17.4131	16.4815
30	27.7941	25.8077	24.0158	22.3965	20.9303	19.6004	18.3920
35	32.0354	29.4086	27.0756	24.9986	23.1452	21.4872	20.0007
40	36.1722	32.8347	29.9158	27.3555	25.1028	23.1148	21.3551
45	40.2072	36.0945	32.5523	29.4902	26.8330	24.5187	22.4955
50	44.1428	39.1961	34.9997	31.4236	28.3623	25.7298	23.4556

TABLE A.4 (CONT.)
PRESENT VALUE OF AN ANNUITY

n\i	4.0%	4.5%	5.0%	5.5%	6.0%	6.5%	7.0%
1	0.9615	0.9569	0.9524	0.9479	0.9434	0.9390	0.9346
2	1.8861	1.8727	1.8594	1.8463	1.8334	1.8206	1.8080
3	2.7751	2.7490	2.7232	2.6979	2.6730	2.6485	2.6243
4	3.6299	3.5875	3.5460	3.5052	3.4651	3.4258	3.3872
5	4.4518	4.3900	4.3295	4.2703	4.2124	4.1557	4.1002
6	5.2421	5.1579	5.0757	4.9955	4.9173	4.8410	4.7665
7	6.0021	5.8927	5.7864	5.6830	5.5824	5.4845	5.3893
8	6.7327	6.5959	6.4632	6.3346	6.2098	6.0888	5.9713
9	7.4353	7.2688	7.1078	6.9522	6.8017	6.6561	6.5152
10	8.1109	7.9127	7.7217	7.5376	7.3601	7.1888	7.0236
11	8.7605	8.5289	8.3064	8.0925	7.8869	7.6890	7.4987
12	9.3851	9.1186	8.8633	8.6185	8.3838	8.1587	7.9427
13	9.9856	9.6829	9.3936	9.1171	8.8527	8.5997	8.3577
14	10.5631	10.2228	9.8986	9.5896	9.2950	9.0138	8.7455
15	11.1184	10.7395	10.3797	10.0376	9.7122	9.4027	9.1079
16	11.6523	11.2340	10.8378	10.4622	10.1059	9.7678	9.4466
17	12.1657	11.7072	11.2741	10.8646	10.4773	10.1106	9.7632
18	12.6593	12.1600	11.6896	11.2461	10.8276	10.4325	10.0591
19	13.1339	12.5933	12.0853	11.6077	11.1581	10.7347	10.3356
20	13.5903	13.0079	12.4622	11.9504	11.4699	11.0185	10.5940
25	15.6221	14.8282	14.0939	13.4139	12.7834	12.1979	11.6536
30	17.2920	16.2889	15.3725	14.5337	13.7648	13.0587	12.4090
35	18.6646	17.4610	16.3742	15.3906	14.4982	13.6870	12.9477
40	19.7928	18.4016	17.1591	16.0461	15.0463	14.1455	13.3317
45	20.7200	19.1563	17.7741	16.5477	15.4558	14.4802	13.6055
50	21.4822	19.7620	18.2559	16.9315	15.7619	14.7245	13.8007

TABLE A.4 (CONT.)
PRESENT VALUE OF AN ANNUITY

n \ i	7.5%	8.0%	8.5%	9.0%	9.5%	10.0%	10.5%
1	0.9302	0.9259	0.9217	0.9174	0.9132	0.9091	0.9050
2	1.7956	1.7833	1.7711	1.7591	1.7473	1.7355	1.7240
3	2.6005	2.5771	2.5540	2.5313	2.5089	2.4869	2.4651
4	3.3493	3.3121	3.2756	3.2397	3.2045	3.1699	3.1359
5	4.0459	3.9927	3.9406	3.8897	3.8397	3.7908	3.7429
6	4.6938	4.6229	4.5536	4.4859	4.4198	4.3553	4.2922
7	5.2966	5.2064	5.1185	5.0330	4.9496	4.8684	4.7893
8	5.8573	5.7466	5.6392	5.5348	5.4334	5.3349	5.2392
9	6.3789	6.2469	6.1191	5.9952	5.8753	5.7590	5.6463
10	6.8641	6.7101	6.5613	6.4177	6.2788	6.1446	6.0148
11	7.3154	7.1390	6.9690	6.8052	6.6473	6.4951	6.3482
12	7.7353	7.5361	7.3447	7.1607	6.9838	6.8137	6.6500
13	8.1258	7.9038	7.6910	7.4869	7.2912	7.1034	6.9230
14	8.4892	8.2442	8.0101	7.7862	7.5719	7.3667	7.1702
15	8.8271	8.5595	8.3042	8.0607	7.8282	7.6061	7.3938
16	9.1415	8.8514	8.5753	8.3126	8.0623	7.8237	7.5962
17	9.4340	9.1216	8.8252	8.5436	8.2760	8.0216	7.7794
18	9.7060	9.3719	9.0555	8.7556	8.4713	8.2014	7.9451
19	9.9591	9.6036	9.2677	8.9501	8.6496	8.3649	8.0952
20	10.1945	9.8181	9.4633	9.1285	8.8124	8.5136	8.2309
25	11.1469	10.6748	10.2342	9.8226	9.4376	9.0770	8.7390
30	11.8104	11.2578	10.7468	10.2737	9.8347	9.4269	9.0474
35	12.2725	11.6546	11.0878	10.5668	10.0870	9.6442	9.2347
40	12.5944	11.9246	11.3145	10.7574	10.2472	9.7791	9.3483
45	12.8186	12.1084	11.4653	10.8812	10.3490	9.8628	9.4173
50	12.9748	12.2335	11.5656	10.9617	10.4137	9.9148	9.4591

TABLE A.4 (CONT.)
PRESENT VALUE OF AN ANNUITY

n\i	11.0%	11.5%	12.0%	12.5%	13.0%	13.5%	14.0%	14.5%
1	0.9009	0.8969	0.8929	0.8889	0.8850	0.8811	0.8772	0.8734
2	1.7125	1.7012	1.6901	1.6790	1.6681	1.6573	1.6467	1.6361
3	2.4437	2.4226	2.4018	2.3813	2.3612	2.3413	2.3216	2.3023
4	3.1024	3.0696	3.0373	3.0056	2.9745	2.9438	2.9137	2.8841
5	3.6959	3.6499	3.6048	3.5606	3.5172	3.4747	3.4331	3.3922
6	4.2305	4.1703	4.1114	4.0538	3.9975	3.9425	3.8887	3.8360
7	4.7122	4.6370	4.5638	4.4923	4.4226	4.3546	4.2883	4.2236
8	5.1461	5.0556	4.9676	4.8820	4.7988	4.7177	4.6389	4.5621
9	5.5370	5.4311	5.3282	5.2285	5.1317	5.0377	4.9464	4.8577
10	5.8892	5.7678	5.6502	5.5364	5.4262	5.3195	5.2161	5.1159
11	6.2065	6.0697	5.9377	5.8102	5.6869	5.5679	5.4527	5.3414
12	6.4924	6.3406	6.1944	6.0535	5.9176	5.7867	5.6603	5.5383
13	6.7499	6.5835	6.4235	6.2698	6.1218	5.9794	5.8424	5.7103
14	6.9819	6.8013	6.6282	6.4620	6.3025	6.1493	6.0021	5.8606
15	7.1909	6.9967	6.8109	6.6329	6.4624	6.2989	6.1422	5.9918
16	7.3792	7.1719	6.9740	6.7848	6.6039	6.4308	6.2651	6.1063
17	7.5488	7.3291	7.1196	6.9198	6.7291	6.5469	6.3729	6.2064
18	7.7016	7.4700	7.2497	7.0398	6.8399	6.6493	6.4674	6.2938
19	7.8393	7.5964	7.3658	7.1465	6.9380	6.7395	6.5504	6.3701
20	7.9633	7.7098	7.4694	7.2414	7.0248	6.8189	6.6231	6.4368
25	8.4217	8.1236	7.8431	7.5790	7.3300	7.0950	6.8729	6.6629
30	8.6938	8.3637	8.0552	7.7664	7.4957	7.2415	7.0027	6.7778
35	8.8552	8.5030	8.1755	7.8704	7.5856	7.3193	7.0700	6.8362
40	8.9511	8.5839	8.2438	7.9281	7.6344	7.3607	7.1050	6.8659
45	9.0079	8.6308	8.2825	7.9601	7.6609	7.3826	7.1232	6.8810
50	9.0417	8.6580	8.3045	7.9778	7.6752	7.3942	7.1327	6.8886

n \ i	15.0%	15.5%	16.0%	16.5%	17.0%	17.5%	18.0%	18.5%
1	0.8696	0.8658	0.8621	0.8584	0.8547	0.8511	0.8475	0.8439
2	1.6257	1.6154	1.6052	1.5952	1.5852	1.5754	1.5656	1.5560
3	2.2832	2.2644	2.2459	2.2276	2.2096	2.1918	2.1743	2.1570
4	2.8550	2.8263	2.7982	2.7705	2.7432	2.7164	2.6901	2.6641
5	3.3522	3.3129	3.2743	3.2365	3.1993	3.1629	3.1272	3.0921
6	3.7845	3.7341	3.6847	3.6365	3.5892	3.5429	3.4976	3.4532
7	4.1604	4.0988	4.0386	3.9798	3.9224	3.8663	3.8115	3.7580
8	4.4873	4.4145	4.3436	4.2745	4.2072	4.1415	4.0776	4.0152
9	4.7716	4.6879	4.6065	4.5275	4.4506	4.3758	4.3030	4.2322
10	5.0188	4.9246	4.8332	4.7446	4.6586	4.5751	4.4941	4.4154
11	5.2337	5.1295	5.0286	4.9310	4.8364	4.7448	4.6560	4.5699
12	5.4206	5.3069	5.1971	5.0910	4.9884	4.8892	4.7932	4.7004
13	5.5831	5.4605	5.3423	5.2283	5.1183	5.0121	4.9095	4.8104
14	5.7245	5.5935	5.4675	5.3462	5.2293	5.1167	5.0081	4.9033
15	5.8474	5.7087	5.5755	5.4474	5.3242	5.2057	5.0916	4.9817
16	5.9542	5.8084	5.6685	5.5342	5.4053	5.2814	5.1624	5.0479
17	6.0472	5.8947	5.7487	5.6088	5.4746	5.3459	5.2223	5.1037
18	6.1280	5.9695	5.8178	5.6728	5.5339	5.4008	5.2732	5.1508
19	6.1982	6.0342	5.8775	5.7277	5.5845	5.4475	5.3162	5.1905
20	6.2593	6.0902	5.9288	5.7748	5.6278	5.4872	5.3527	5.2241
25	6.4641	6.2758	6.0971	5.9274	5.7662	5.6129	5.4669	5.3278
30	6.5660	6.3661	6.1772	5.9986	5.8294	5.6690	5.5168	5.3722
35	6.6166	6.4100	6.2153	6.0317	5.8582	5.6941	5.5386	5.3912
40	6.6418	6.4314	6.2335	6.0471	5.8713	5.7053	5.5482	5.3993
45	6.6543	6.4418	6.2421	6.0543	5.8773	5.7103	5.5523	5.4028
50	6.6605	6.4468	6.2463	6.0577	5.8801	5.7125	5.5541	5.4043

TABLE A.4 (CONT.)
PRESENT VALUE OF AN ANNUITY

n \ i	19.0%	19.5%	20.0%	20.5%	21.0%	21.5%	22.0%	22.5%
1	0.8403	0.8368	0.8333	0.8299	0.8264	0.8230	0.8197	0.8163
2	1.5465	1.5371	1.5278	1.5186	1.5095	1.5004	1.4915	1.4827
3	2.1399	2.1231	2.1065	2.0901	2.0739	2.0580	2.0422	2.0267
4	2.6386	2.6135	2.5887	2.5644	2.5404	2.5169	2.4936	2.4708
5	3.0576	3.0238	2.9906	2.9580	2.9260	2.8945	2.8636	2.8333
6	3.4098	3.3672	3.3255	3.2847	3.2446	3.2054	3.1669	3.1292
7	3.7057	3.6546	3.6046	3.5557	3.5079	3.4612	3.4155	3.3708
8	3.9544	3.8950	3.8372	3.7807	3.7256	3.6718	3.6193	3.5680
9	4.1633	4.0963	4.0310	3.9674	3.9054	3.8451	3.7863	3.7290
10	4.3389	4.2647	4.1925	4.1223	4.0541	3.9877	3.9232	3.8604
11	4.4865	4.4056	4.3271	4.2509	4.1769	4.1051	4.0354	3.9677
12	4.6105	4.5235	4.4392	4.3576	4.2784	4.2017	4.1274	4.0552
13	4.7147	4.6222	4.5327	4.4461	4.3624	4.2813	4.2028	4.1267
14	4.8023	4.7047	4.6106	4.5196	4.4317	4.3467	4.2646	4.1851
15	4.8759	4.7738	4.6755	4.5806	4.4890	4.4006	4.3152	4.2327
16	4.9377	4.8317	4.7296	4.6312	4.5364	4.4449	4.3567	4.2716
17	4.9897	4.8801	4.7746	4.6732	4.5755	4.4814	4.3908	4.3034
18	5.0333	4.9205	4.8122	4.7080	4.6079	4.5115	4.4187	4.3293
19	5.0700	4.9544	4.8435	4.7370	4.6346	4.5362	4.4415	4.3504
20	5.1009	4.9828	4.8696	4.7610	4.6567	4.5565	4.4603	4.3677
25	5.1951	5.0685	4.9476	4.8320	4.7213	4.6154	4.5139	4.4166
30	5.2347	5.1037	4.9789	4.8599	4.7463	4.6377	4.5338	4.4344
35	5.2512	5.1182	4.9915	4.8709	4.7559	4.6461	4.5411	4.4408
40	5.2582	5.1241	4.9966	4.8752	4.7596	4.6492	4.5439	4.4431
45	5.2611	5.1265	4.9986	4.8769	4.7610	4.6504	4.5449	4.4440
50	5.2623	5.1275	4.9995	4.8776	4.7616	4.6509	4.5452	4.4443

```
---------------------------------------------------------------
TABLE A.4 (CONCLUDED)
PRESENT VALUE OF AN ANNUITY
---------------------------------------------------------------
```

n\i	23.0%	23.5%	24.0%	24.5%	25.0%
1	0.8130	0.8097	0.8065	0.8032	0.8000
2	1.4740	1.4654	1.4568	1.4484	1.4400
3	2.0114	1.9962	1.9813	1.9666	1.9520
4	2.4483	2.4261	2.4043	2.3828	2.3616
5	2.8035	2.7742	2.7454	2.7171	2.6893
6	3.0923	3.0560	3.0205	2.9856	2.9514
7	3.3270	3.2842	3.2423	3.2013	3.1611
8	3.5179	3.4690	3.4212	3.3745	3.3289
9	3.6731	3.6186	3.5655	3.5137	3.4631
10	3.7993	3.7398	3.6819	3.6254	3.5705
11	3.9018	3.8379	3.7757	3.7152	3.6564
12	3.9852	3.9173	3.8514	3.7873	3.7251
13	4.0530	3.9816	3.9124	3.8452	3.7801
14	4.1082	4.0337	3.9616	3.8918	3.8241
15	4.1530	4.0759	4.0013	3.9291	3.8593
16	4.1894	4.1100	4.0333	3.9591	3.8874
17	4.2190	4.1377	4.0591	3.9832	3.9099
18	4.2431	4.1601	4.0799	4.0026	3.9279
19	4.2627	4.1782	4.0967	4.0182	3.9424
20	4.2786	4.1929	4.1103	4.0306	3.9539
25	4.3232	4.2336	4.1474	4.0646	3.9849
30	4.3391	4.2478	4.1601	4.0759	3.9950
35	4.3447	4.2527	4.1644	4.0797	3.9984
40	4.3467	4.2544	4.1659	4.0810	3.9995
45	4.3474	4.2550	4.1664	4.0814	3.9998
50	4.3477	4.2552	4.1666	4.0816	3.9999

APPENDIX B

KEYSTROKES FOR SOLVING SELECTED TVM PROBLEMS
USING THE HP–12C CALCULATOR

Note: The individual keystrokes listed in this appendix are separated by commas.

1. Preliminary "housekeeping" and miscellaneous chores

    a. Clearing memory

        yellow f, REG or
        yellow f, FIN

    b. Setting number of decimal places

        yellow f and desired number

    c. Clearing display or eliminating last keystroke

        CLX

    d. Raising a number to a power

        base number, ENTER, exponent, y^x

2. Future value of a single sum problems

    a. Finding FVSS

        amount of present value, CHS, PV, number of periods, n, interest rate, i, FV

    b. Finding approximate n

        amount of present value, CHS, PV, amount of future value, FV, interest rate, i, n

    c. Finding i

        amount of present value, CHS, PV, amount of future value, FV, number of periods, n, i

3. Present value of a single sum problems

    a. Finding PVSS

        amount of future value, FV, number of periods, n, interest rate, i, PV

    b. Finding approximate n

        see 2.b. above

c. Finding i

    see 2.c. above

4. Future value of an annuity problems

a. Finding FVA

    amount of one payment, CHS, PMT, interest rate, i, number of payments, n, blue g, END, FV

b. Finding approximate n

    future value of the annuity, FV, amount of one payment, CHS, PMT, blue g, END, interest rate, i, n

c. Finding i

    future value of the annuity, FV, amount of one payment, CHS, PMT, number of payments, n, blue g, END, i

5. Future value of an annuity due problems

a. Finding FVAD

    amount of one payment, CHS, PMT, interest rate, i, number of payments, n, blue g, BEG, FV

b. Finding approximate n

    future value of the annuity due, FV, amount of one payment, CHS, PMT, blue g, BEG, interest rate, i, n

c. Finding i

    future value of the annuity due, FV, amount of one payment, CHS, PMT, number of payments, n, blue g, BEG, i

6. Sinking fund problems

a. Finding sinking fund payment

    target amount of sinking fund, FV, interest rate, i, number of payments, n, blue g, BEG (or END), PMT

b. Finding approximate n

    target amount of sinking fund, FV, interest rate, i, amount of one payment, CHS, PMT, blue g, BEG (or END), n

c. Finding i

> target amount of sinking fund, FV, amount of one payment, CHS, PMT, number of payments, n, blue g, BEG (or END), i

7. Present value of an annuity problems

   a. Finding PVA

   > amount of one payment, CHS, PMT, interest rate, i, number of payments, n, blue g, END, PV

   b. Finding approximate n

   > present value of the annuity, CHS, PV, amount of one payment, PMT, blue g, END, interest rate, i, n

   c. Finding i

   > present value of the annuity, CHS, PV, amount of one payment, PMT, number of payments, n, blue g, END, i

8. Present value of an annuity due problems

   a. Finding PVAD

   > amount of one payment, CHS, PMT, interest rate, i, number of payments, n, blue g, BEG, PV

   b. Finding approximate n

   > present value of the annuity due, CHS, PV, amount of one payment, PMT, blue g, BEG, interest rate, i, n

   c. Finding i

   > present value of the annuity due, CHS, PV, amount of one payment, PMT, number of payments, n, blue g, BEG, i

9. Debt service/capital sum liquidation problems

   a. Finding the payment

   > beginning amount of loan or capital sum, CHS, PV, interest rate, i, number of payments, n, blue g, BEG (or END), PMT

   b. Finding the approximate n

   > beginning amount of loan or capital sum, CHS, PV, interest rate, i, amount of one payment, PMT, blue g, BEG (or END), n

c. Finding i

      beginning amount of loan or capital sum, CHS, PV, amount of one payment, PMT, number of payments, n, blue g, BEG (or END), i

d. Creating an amortization schedule

      annual interest rate, i (or blue g, 12 ÷ if loan payments are to be made monthly), blue g, END (normally), beginning amount of loan, PV, amount of one loan payment, CHS, PMT, 1 (or 12 if loan payments are to be made monthly), yellow f, AMORT (to show total interest payments in first year), x≷y (to show total principal payments in first year), RCL, PV (to show unpaid loan balance at end of first year); repeat 1 (or 12), yellow f, AMORT, x ≷y, RCL, PV to show the total interest payments, principal payments, and unpaid loan balance for each successive year of the loan's duration.

10. Present value of uneven cash flows problems

a. Cash flows at end of year: ungrouped data (see text for grouped data)

      amount of first cash flow, blue g, CFj, second cash flow, blue g, CFj, etc. through entire sequence; then interest rate, i, yellow f, NPV

b. Cash flows at beginning of year: ungrouped data (see text for grouped data)

      amount of first cash flow, blue g, CFo, second cash flow, blue g, CFj, third cash flow, blue g, CFj, etc. through entire sequence; then interest rate, i, yellow f, NPV

c. Cash flows that grow by a constant percentage, with first payment made immediately

      blue g, BEG, amount of first cash flow, PMT, 1 plus interest rate, ENTER, 1 plus growth rate, ÷, 1, −, 100, x, i, number of years, n, PV

d. Cash flows that grow by a constant percentage, with first payment made after one year

      divide answer found in 10 c. by (1 plus interest rate)

11. Future value of uneven cash flows problems

a. Generally

      Compute present value as in 10.a. or b. above; then ENTER, CHS, PV, interest rate, i, number of years, n, FV

b. Special case: deposits growing by a constant percentage

      Compute present value as in 10.c. or d. above; then STO, 1, yellow f, FIN, RCL, 1, PV, interest rate, i, number of years, n, FV

12. Net present value problems

    a. Ungrouped data

        amount of initial outflow, CHS, blue g, CFo; then amount of each succeeding inflow or outflow, including zeros, pressing blue g and CFj after each (CHS, blue g, and CFj for outflows); then interest rate, i, yellow f, NPV

    b. Grouped data

        amount of initial outflow, CHS, blue g, CFo; then amount of first inflow or outflow, including zeros, blue g, CFj (CHS, blue g, CFj for outflows); then number of times that amount occurs in succession, blue g, Nj; repeat the process for each subsequent inflow, outflow, or zero flow or group of same; then interest rate, i, yellow f, NPV

13. Internal rate of return problems

    Same as NPV except for last four keystrokes; instead of interest rate, i, yellow f, NPV, press yellow f, IRR

14. Conversion of nominal interest rate to effective interest rate problems

    a. Discrete compounding or discounting

        nominal interest rate, ENTER, number of compounding periods per year, n, $\div$, i, 100, CHS, ENTER, PV, FV, +

    b. Continuous compounding or discounting during 360–day year

        1, ENTER, nominal interest rate, %, blue g, e^x, Δ%

APPENDIX C

KEYSTROKES FOR SOLVING SELECTED TVM PROBLEMS
USING THE BA-II CALCULATOR

Note: The individual keystrokes in this appendix are separated by commas.

1. Preliminary "housekeeping"

   a. Entering the finance function mode

      2nd, Mode (once or twice till FIN appears)

   b. Clearing display or eliminating last keystroke

      ON/C

   c. Clearing memory

      2nd, CMR

   d. Setting number of decimal places

      FIX and desired number

   e. Raising a number to a power

      base number, 2nd, y^x, exponent, =

2. Future value of a single sum problems

   a. Finding FVSS

      amount of present value, PV, number of periods, N, interest rate, %i, 2nd, FV

   b. Finding n

      amount of present value, PV, amount of future value, FV, interest rate, %i, 2nd, N

   c. Finding i

      amount of present value, PV, amount of future value, FV, number of periods, N, 2nd, %i

3. Present value of a single sum problems

   a. Finding PVSS

      amount of future value, FV, number of periods, N, interest rate, %i, 2nd, PV

b. Finding n

    see 2.b. above

c. Finding i

    see 2.c. above

4. Future value of an annuity problems

  a. Finding FVA

    amount of one payment, PMT, interest rate, %i, number of payments, N, 2nd, FV

  b. Finding n

    future value of the annuity, FV, amount of one payment, PMT, interest rate, %i, 2nd, N

  c. Finding i

    future value of the annuity, FV, amount of one payment, PMT, number of payments, N, 2nd, %i

5. Future value of an annuity due problems

  a. Finding FVAD

    amount of one payment, PMT, interest rate, %i, number of payments, N, DUE, FV

  b. Finding n

    future value of the annuity due, FV, amount of one payment, PMT, interest rate, %i, DUE, N

  c. Finding i

    future value of the annuity due, FV, amount of one payment, PMT, number of payments, N, DUE, %i

6. Sinking fund problems

  a. Finding sinking fund payment

    target amount of sinking fund, FV, interest rate, %i, number of payments, N, DUE, (or 2nd), PMT

  b. Finding n

    target amount of sinking fund, FV, interest rate, %i, amount of one payment, PMT, DUE (or 2nd), N

c. Finding i

   target amount of sinking fund, FV, amount of one payment, PMT, number of payments, N, DUE (or 2nd), %i

7. Present value of an annuity problems

   a. Finding PVA

      amount of one payment, PMT, interest rate, %i, number of payments, N, 2nd, PV

   b. Finding n

      present value of the annuity, PV, amount of one payment, PMT, interest rate, %i, 2nd, N

   c. Finding i

      present value of the annuity, PV, amount of one payment, PMT, number of payments, N, 2nd, %i

8. Present value of an annuity due problems

   a. Finding PVAD

      amount of one payment, PMT, interest rate, %i, number of payments, N, DUE, PV

   b. Finding n

      present value of the annuity due, PV, amount of one payment, PMT, interest rate, %i, DUE, N

   c. Finding i

      present value of the annuity due, PV, amount of one payment, PMT, number of payments, N, DUE, %i

9. Debt service/capital sum liquidation problems

   a. Finding the payment

      beginning amount of loan or capital sum, PV, interest rate, %i, number of payments, N, DUE (or 2nd), PMT

   b. Finding n

      beginning amount of loan or capital sum, PV, interest rate, %i, amount of one payment, PMT, DUE (or 2nd), N

c. Finding i

  beginning amount of loan or capital sum, PV, amount of one payment, PMT, number of payments, N, DUE (or 2nd), %i

d. Creating an amortization schedule

  beginning amount of loan, PV, amount of one payment, PMT, number of payments, N, interest rate, %i, 1, 2nd, P/I (to show principal payment), x$\lessgtr$y (to show interest amount); for subsequent years, 2, 2nd, P/I, x$\lessgtr$y, 3, 2nd, P/I, x$\lessgtr$y, 4, 2nd, P/I,2 x$\lessgtr$y, etc.

10. Present value of uneven cash flows that grow by a constant percentage

  a. First payment is made immediately

  amount of first payment, PMT, 1 plus interest rate, ÷, 1 plus growth rate, −, 1, x, 100, =, %i, number of years, N, DUE, PV

  b. First payment is made after one year

  divide answer found in 10.a. by (1 plus interest rate)

11. Future value of uneven cash flows that grow by a constant percentage

  Compute present value as in 10.a. or b. above; then STO, 2nd, CMR, RCL, PV, interest rate, %i, number of years, N, 2nd, FV

12. Conversion of nominal interest rate to effective interest rate problems

  a. Discrete compounding or discounting

  number of compounding periods per year, N, nominal interest rate, ÷, number of compounding periods per year, =, %i, 1, PV, 2nd, FV, 1, N, 2nd, %i

  b. Continuous compounding or discounting during 360-day year

  nominal interest rate, %, 2nd, e^x, −, 1, =, x, 100, =

APPENDIX D

TABLE OF EFFECTIVE INTEREST RATES

TABLE D.1

EFFECTIVE ANNUAL INTEREST RATES

NOMINAL ANNUAL	COMPOUNDING		FREQUENCY			
INTEREST RATE	SEMI-ANNUALLY	QUAR-TERLY	MONTHLY	WEEKLY	DAILY (360)	CONTINUOUS (360)
0.25%	0.25016%	0.25023%	0.25029%	0.25031%	0.25031%	0.25031%
0.50%	0.50063%	0.50094%	0.50115%	0.50123%	0.50125%	0.50125%
0.75%	0.75141%	0.75211%	0.75258%	0.75277%	0.75281%	0.75282%
1.00%	1.00250%	1.00376%	1.00460%	1.00492%	1.00500%	1.00502%
1.25%	1.25391%	1.25587%	1.25719%	1.25769%	1.25782%	1.25785%
1.50%	1.50562%	1.50846%	1.51036%	1.51109%	1.51127%	1.51131%
1.75%	1.75766%	1.76152%	1.76410%	1.76510%	1.76536%	1.76540%
2.00%	2.01000%	2.01505%	2.01844%	2.01974%	2.02008%	2.02013%
2.25%	2.26266%	2.26906%	2.27335%	2.27501%	2.27543%	2.27550%
2.50%	2.51562%	2.52354%	2.52885%	2.53090%	2.53142%	2.53151%
2.75%	2.76891%	2.77849%	2.78493%	2.78741%	2.78805%	2.78816%
3.00%	3.02250%	3.03392%	3.04160%	3.04456%	3.04532%	3.04545%
3.25%	3.27641%	3.28982%	3.29885%	3.30234%	3.30324%	3.30339%
3.50%	3.53063%	3.54621%	3.55670%	3.56075%	3.56179%	3.56197%
3.75%	3.78516%	3.80306%	3.81513%	3.81980%	3.82100%	3.82120%
4.00%	4.04000%	4.06040%	4.07415%	4.07948%	4.08085%	4.08108%
4.25%	4.29516%	4.31822%	4.33377%	4.33979%	4.34134%	4.34161%
4.50%	4.55063%	4.57651%	4.59398%	4.60075%	4.60249%	4.60279%
4.75%	4.80641%	4.83528%	4.85479%	4.86235%	4.86429%	4.86462%
5.00%	5.06250%	5.09453%	5.11619%	5.12458%	5.12674%	5.12711%
5.25%	5.31891%	5.35427%	5.37819%	5.38747%	5.38985%	5.39026%
5.50%	5.57562%	5.61448%	5.64079%	5.65099%	5.65362%	5.65406%
5.75%	5.83266%	5.87518%	5.90398%	5.91516%	5.91804%	5.91853%
6.00%	6.09000%	6.13636%	6.16778%	6.17998%	6.18312%	6.18365%
6.25%	6.34766%	6.39802%	6.43218%	6.44545%	6.44887%	6.44945%
6.50%	6.60562%	6.66016%	6.69719%	6.71157%	6.71528%	6.71590%
6.75%	6.86391%	6.92279%	6.96279%	6.97834%	6.98235%	6.98303%
7.00%	7.12250%	7.18590%	7.22901%	7.24577%	7.25009%	7.25082%

EFFECTIVE ANNUAL INTEREST RATES

NOMINAL ANNUAL INTEREST RATE	COMPOUNDING			FREQUENCY		
	SEMI-ANNUALLY	QUAR-TERLY	MONTHLY	WEEKLY	DAILY (360)	CONTINUOUS (360)
7.25%	7.38141%	7.44950%	7.49583%	7.51385%	7.51850%	7.51928%
7.50%	7.64063%	7.71359%	7.76326%	7.78259%	7.78757%	7.78842%
7.75%	7.90016%	7.97816%	8.03130%	8.05199%	8.05732%	8.05822%
8.00%	8.16000%	8.24322%	8.29995%	8.32205%	8.32774%	8.32871%
8.25%	8.42016%	8.50876%	8.56921%	8.59277%	8.59884%	8.59987%
8.50%	8.68062%	8.77480%	8.83909%	8.86415%	8.87061%	8.87171%
8.75%	8.94141%	9.04132%	9.10958%	9.13620%	9.14307%	9.14423%
9.00%	9.20250%	9.30833%	9.38069%	9.40892%	9.41620%	9.41743%
9.25%	9.46391%	9.57583%	9.65241%	9.68230%	9.69001%	9.69131%
9.50%	9.72563%	9.84383%	9.92476%	9.95635%	9.96451%	9.96589%
9.75%	9.98766%	10.11231%	10.19772%	10.23108%	10.23969%	10.24114%
10.00%	10.25000%	10.38129%	10.47131%	10.50648%	10.51556%	10.51709%
10.25%	10.51266%	10.65076%	10.74551%	10.78255%	10.79211%	10.79373%
10.50%	10.77563%	10.92072%	11.02035%	11.05930%	11.06936%	11.07106%
10.75%	11.03891%	11.19118%	11.29580%	11.33673%	11.34730%	11.34909%
11.00%	11.30250%	11.46213%	11.57188%	11.61484%	11.62593%	11.62781%
11.25%	11.56641%	11.73357%	11.84859%	11.89363%	11.90526%	11.90723%
11.50%	11.83063%	12.00551%	12.12593%	12.17310%	12.18528%	12.18734%
11.75%	12.09516%	12.27795%	12.40390%	12.45326%	12.46601%	12.46816%
12.00%	12.36000%	12.55088%	12.68250%	12.73410%	12.74743%	12.74969%
12.25%	12.62516%	12.82431%	12.96174%	13.01563%	13.02956%	13.03191%
12.50%	12.89063%	13.09824%	13.24160%	13.29785%	13.31239%	13.31485%
12.75%	13.15641%	13.37267%	13.52211%	13.58076%	13.59592%	13.59849%
13.00%	13.42250%	13.64759%	13.80325%	13.86436%	13.88017%	13.88284%
13.25%	13.68891%	13.92302%	14.08503%	14.14866%	14.16512%	14.16790%
13.50%	13.95563%	14.19894%	14.36744%	14.43366%	14.45078%	14.45368%
13.75%	14.22266%	14.47537%	14.65050%	14.71935%	14.73716%	14.74017%
14.00%	14.49000%	14.75230%	14.93420%	15.00574%	15.02425%	15.02738%

D.3

EFFECTIVE ANNUAL INTEREST RATES

NOMINAL ANNUAL INTEREST RATE	COMPOUNDING FREQUENCY					
	SEMI-ANNUALLY	QUAR-TERLY	MONTHLY	WEEKLY	DAILY (360)	CONTINUOUS (360)
14.25%	14.75766%	15.02973%	15.21855%	15.29284%	15.31206%	15.31531%
14.50%	15.02563%	15.30766%	15.50354%	15.58063%	15.60058%	15.60396%
14.75%	15.29391%	15.58610%	15.78917%	15.86913%	15.88983%	15.89333%
15.00%	15.56250%	15.86504%	16.07545%	16.15834%	16.17979%	16.18342%
15.25%	15.83141%	16.14449%	16.36238%	16.44825%	16.47049%	16.47425%
15.50%	16.10063%	16.42444%	16.64996%	16.73888%	16.76190%	16.76580%
15.75%	16.37016%	16.70489%	16.93820%	17.03021%	17.05404%	17.05808%
16.00%	16.64000%	16.98586%	17.22708%	17.32226%	17.34692%	17.35109%
16.25%	16.91016%	17.26733%	17.51662%	17.61503%	17.64052%	17.64483%
16.50%	17.18062%	17.54930%	17.80681%	17.90851%	17.93485%	17.93931%
16.75%	17.45141%	17.83179%	18.09766%	18.20271%	18.22992%	18.23453%
17.00%	17.72250%	18.11478%	18.38917%	18.49762%	18.52573%	18.53048%
17.25%	17.99391%	18.39829%	18.68134%	18.79326%	18.82227%	18.82718%
17.50%	18.26562%	18.68230%	18.97417%	19.08963%	19.11956%	19.12462%
17.75%	18.53766%	18.96682%	19.26766%	19.38671%	19.41758%	19.42281%
18.00%	18.81000%	19.25186%	19.56182%	19.68453%	19.71635%	19.72174%
18.25%	19.08266%	19.53741%	19.85664%	19.98307%	20.01587%	20.02141%
18.50%	19.35563%	19.82347%	20.15212%	20.28235%	20.31613%	20.32184%
18.75%	19.62891%	20.11004%	20.44828%	20.58235%	20.61714%	20.62302%
19.00%	19.90250%	20.39713%	20.74510%	20.88309%	20.91890%	20.92496%
19.25%	20.17641%	20.68473%	21.04259%	21.18457%	21.22141%	21.22765%
19.50%	20.45063%	20.97285%	21.34076%	21.48678%	21.52468%	21.53110%
19.75%	20.72516%	21.26148%	21.63960%	21.78973%	21.82871%	21.83531%
20.00%	21.00000%	21.55063%	21.93911%	22.09343%	22.13349%	22.14028%
20.25%	21.27516%	21.84029%	22.23930%	22.39786%	22.43904%	22.44601%
20.50%	21.55063%	22.13047%	22.54016%	22.70304%	22.74534%	22.75251%
20.75%	21.82641%	22.42117%	22.84171%	23.00897%	23.05242%	23.05977%
21.00%	22.10250%	22.71239%	23.14393%	23.31564%	23.36025%	23.36781%

EFFECTIVE ANNUAL INTEREST RATES

NOMINAL ANNUAL INTEREST RATE	COMPOUNDING	FREQUENCY				
	SEMI- ANNUALLY	QUAR- TERLY	MONTHLY	WEEKLY	DAILY (360)	CONTINUOUS (360)
21.25%	22.37891%	23.00413%	23.44684%	23.62307%	23.66886%	23.67661%
21.50%	22.65563%	23.29639%	23.75043%	23.93125%	23.97823%	23.98619%
21.75%	22.93266%	23.58917%	24.05470%	24.24017%	24.28838%	24.29654%
22.00%	23.21000%	23.88247%	24.35966%	24.54986%	24.59930%	24.60767%
22.25%	23.48766%	24.17629%	24.66530%	24.86030%	24.91100%	24.91958%
22.50%	23.76562%	24.47063%	24.97164%	25.17150%	25.22347%	25.23227%
22.75%	24.04391%	24.76550%	25.27866%	25.48346%	25.53672%	25.54574%
23.00%	24.32250%	25.06089%	25.58638%	25.79619%	25.85076%	25.86000%
23.25%	24.60141%	25.35680%	25.89479%	26.10967%	26.16558%	26.17504%
23.50%	24.88063%	25.65324%	26.20389%	26.42393%	26.48118%	26.49088%
23.75%	25.16016%	25.95021%	26.51368%	26.73895%	26.79757%	26.80750%
24.00%	25.44000%	26.24770%	26.82418%	27.05474%	27.11475%	27.12491%
24.25%	25.72016%	26.54571%	27.13537%	27.37131%	27.43272%	27.44312%
24.50%	26.00063%	26.84426%	27.44727%	27.68864%	27.75149%	27.76213%
24.75%	26.28141%	27.14333%	27.75986%	28.00676%	28.07104%	28.08194%
25.00%	26.56250%	27.44293%	28.07316%	28.32565%	28.39140%	28.40254%